A

TROSTREY

CHILDHOOD

GRAHAM HARRIS

Published by Saron Publishing in 2021

Copyright © 2021

ISBN-13: 978-1-913297-20-6

Cover design by © 2021 Tassam Design

Saron Publishers
Pwllmeyrick House
Mamhilad
Mon
NP4 8RG

www.saronpublishers.co.uk
info@saronpublishers.co.uk
Follow us on Facebook and Twitter

DEDICATION

To all the good old country folk who just get on with it

Life, that is

CONTENTS

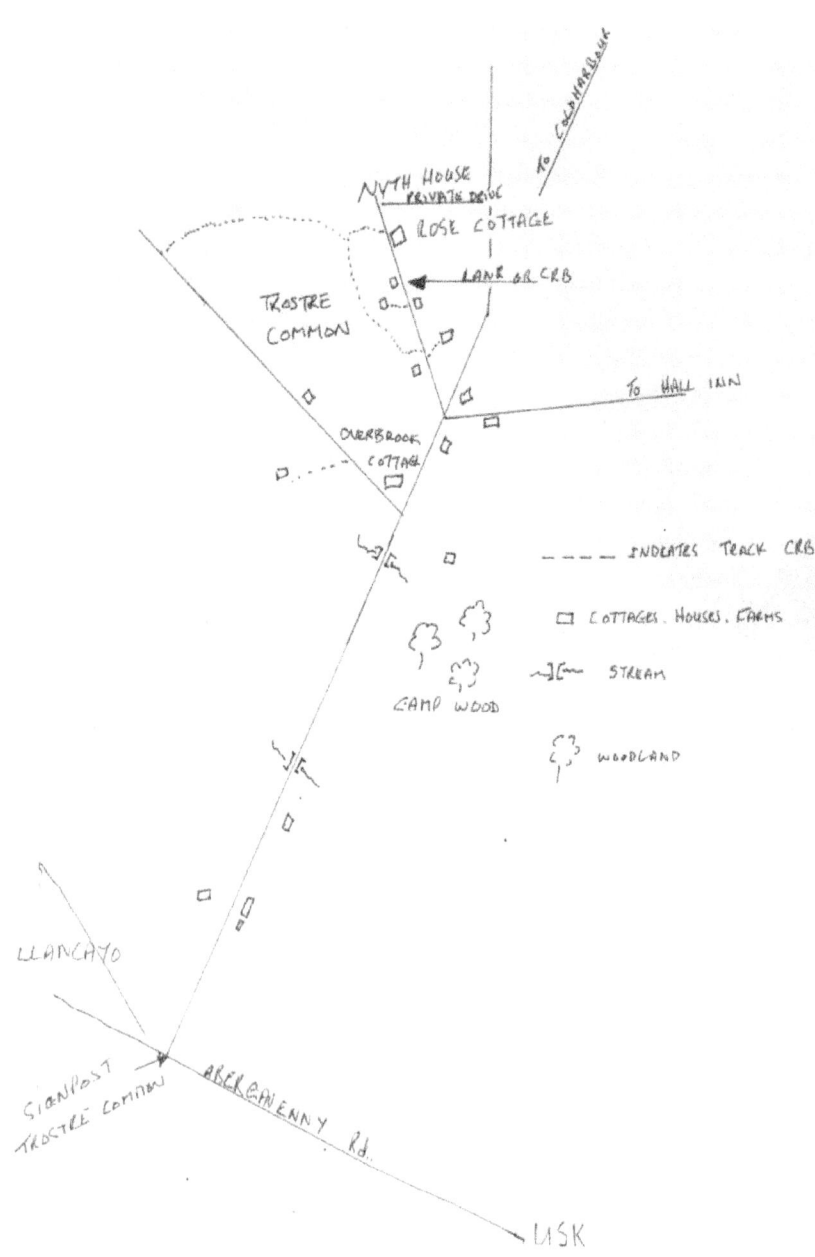

MYTH HOUSE
PRIVATE DRIVE

To COLD-HARBOUR

ROSE COTTAGE

LANE or CRB

TROSTRE
COMMON

To HALL INN

OVERBROOK
COTTAGE

- - - - INDICATES TRACK CRB

☐ COTTAGES. HOUSES. FARMS

STREAM

CAMP WOOD

WOODLAND

LLANCAYO

SIGNPOST
TROSTRE COMMON

ABERGANENNY Rd.

USK

6

Chapter 1 Trostrey

Trostrey Common can fairly be described as a hamlet, situated in Monmouthshire in the south-east corner of Wales. Very little of the actual Common is now left, approximately just an acre at the bottom of a lane off the Usk to Chainbridge road, near Llancayo. This lane leads to four cottages. The area has scattered cottages and houses, with a predominance of farms. Set on the side of a hill, the lane carries on over the brow of the hill until it reaches the main Usk to Raglan road, though there are endless twisting lanes branching off the main lane, so typical of rural areas in Wales.

Once you turn off the Usk-Chainbridge road, you go up a lane and past Overbrook Cottage where Uncle Ern and Auntie Minnie lived. Going off to your left, there is a small track more or less opposite the cottage. There were, at one time, four cottages along this track. The locals had a rhyme which summed up the cottages' positions and notoriety:

Magpie Roost
Primrose Pen
Smokey Hole
and Devils Den

Magpie Roost - because the cottage was in woodland.

Primrose Pen - because the cottage was situated on a sunny bank where primroses grew in large numbers.

Smokey Hole – because of its location, the west wind was always driving the smoke back down the chimney.

Devils Den (Overbrook) – So called because a lot of homemade wine was made and consumed there. One of the specialities was homemade elderberry wine but from an elderberry bush which produced white elderberries. There are still white elderberries growing around there today. I don't think the taste or strength was enhanced or impaired

Overbrook in 2020

by the colour of the fruit! Wine was made from any plant, fruit, berry which could be gathered or grown.

Two of the cottages were derelict. Smokey Hole and Devils Den are still lived in!

The bottom end of the Common on the right-hand side going up was once the site of a cockfighting pit, allegedly the last in Monmouthshire. I believe the late Gwyn Davies of The Haven, Trostrey had evidence of this cockfighting activity. Hopefully, his sons are still in possession of this evidence. One of the cottages up the lane was called Cockfighters Tump (Now Yew Tree, previously Canterbury Castle).

Other points of interest along the lane include one of the few sites in Monmouthshire where mistletoe *(Viscum album)* is found growing on oak, *(Quercus robur)*, on what was the site of the 'old well' which supplied water to the four cottages. Less than half a dozen recorded sites of mistletoe growing on oak now exist. At least two have been lost, either to felling or wind damage. Other interesting things included the Elderflower *(Sambucus nigra)* with white berries, and further up the lane was a great site for glow-worms *(Lampyris noctiluca)*.

The Still House belonged to Hill Farm, Trostrey. It was so called because it was the last site in Monmouthshire where illegal liquor production took place. The people who undertook this production were the last in the county to be transported to Australia.[1] The cottage is in a prime position, quite remote, and one could only get to it by walking. It was supplied with running water by means of a small stream and an equally small pond. I understand when the contents and machinery were sold off at Hill Farm a few years ago, Henry Humphreys of Usk Castle purchased the still which still had holes in its side which the Custom and Excise officers had driven in with iron bars to render it useless. I understand the Still is still at Usk Castle as point of interest.[2]

Chapter 2 Family History

My family has lived in the area for generations. My maternal grandfather, William Parker, lived at Weir Cottage, near Llancayo, the first cottage on your right from Usk just after the Trostrey Church signpost. He was the river warden and his beat was from Newbridge-on-Usk to Chain Bridge, a stretch of about eight miles. His 'office' was The Three Salmons Hotel in Usk. My mother Winifred was born and raised at Weir Cottage.

As a child, one of my mother's tasks was to row 'the old toffs' across the river by the weir. The payment for this task was sixpence (2½p in today's money - worth about £1.50)! Mother always told us to watch out for the 'Old Toffs' as they would try and palm you off with a 'silver joey', a silver threepenny bit, which was only worth half of a sixpence. Both coins were very similar but the threepenny coin was a bit smaller.

Grandpa Parker, with bowler, cane and large moustache outside the Three Salmons in Usk

In March 1913, Grandfather Parker died in an incident near his home. In April 1913, the *Usk Advertiser* carried the following:

Water Bailiff Drowned at Usk

On March 20th, a good deal of excitement was aroused at Usk, by a rumour, which subsequently proved to be well founded, that Mr WH Parker of Trostrey Weir, was drowned. The finding of his walking stick in a gap in the fence, near the Long Bridge, and the fact that he had not been home since the previous Monday, raised grave suspicions, and the police made a search along the bank of the river, with the result that his body was found in the river, about 50 yards below the spot

11

where the stick was found. The deceased was about 57 years of age and had been a water bailiff for about 30 years. He was one of the most popular and well known of the officials. A widow, four sons and five daughters are left. An inquest was held at the Sessions House, on March 28th, before Mr Bickerton H Deakin. Councillor EJ Smith was appointed foreman of the jury.

Amy Parker, widow, said deceased went from home, on duty, at 2 o'clock in the afternoon on Easter Monday, and did not return. She knew nothing of the circumstances connected with his death. He was 59 next birthday and was employed as a water bailiff, by the Boards of Conservators.

John Halliday, water bailiff, stated that he saw the deceased about 10.45pm. he had just finished his round. He saw him at the Three Salmons, where he had called to see some fishing gentleman. It was part of their duty to give fishermen any information they required concerning the state of the river. He and Parker left the Hotel together and walked up the Abergavenny Road, towards Trostrey Weir. Witness lived in Usk.

The Coroner: Why did you walk with him when you were off duty?

Witness: We are never off duty.

Continuing, witness said he went up the road with Parker to have a talk. They parted about half a mile from the town and Parker proceeded towards home. They left the Salmons about 10.55 and when he left Parker it would be about 11.30. They had walked slowly and were sometimes standing. It was a very dark night. Parker would not have had to leave the road to reach home, unless he wished to

*follow the river. He had heard that a walking
stick belonging to deceased had been found on
the bank of the river. That was found about
200 yards from where he left him. The stick
was produced and witness recognised it as
belonging to Parker.*

*The Coroner: How would he get to the river
bank?*

*Witness: The fence at this spot is broken down
and it is a very dangerous place. He could have
walked off the road by accident, or he might
have heard something and gone to find out
what it was. The body was found about 20
yards below the spot where the stick was
found. The bank of the river is steep just here
and the water deep – he should think five or six
feet.*

*The Coroner was again asking witness as to
the hours of duty, when Captain Phillips, as
superintendent water bailiff, explained that the
men might be on duty at any hour. There were
absolutely no fixed hours.*

*Halliday further stated that if Parker had
heard any noise which aroused his suspicions,
it would be his duty to go to see what it was. In
answer to a juryman, witness said it was
practically level from the footpath to the edge
of the river and there was no fence whatever.
It would be easy to miss the road and walk into
the river.*

*Rev JG Williams: What was Parker's
condition?*

Witness: He was sober, sir.

*John Pitt, senior, gave evidence as to finding
the stick on the Tuesday morning. It was
leaning against a bush of thorns near the
broken-down wooden fence. He examined the
place but has no idea what had happened. On*

the Wednesday morning he showed PS Sheddick where he found the stick and they tracked the footmarks down to the river. They could also see finger marks where someone had struggled to get up the bank. The distance from the edge of the footpath to the bank was 15 feet. Any man might easily stumble into the river at this spot.

PS Sheddick stated that he received information that Parker was missing, on Tuesday afternoon. He made enquiries and also searched the river banks but found nothing. He corroborated the evidence of the previous witness as to the marks he subsequently found on the bank. He went to get something to search the water with and on returning the body had just been taken from the river by PC John Williams and Mr Fred Lewis. He recognised the body as that of Parker. He did not see any marks of violence, with the exception of a few slight scratches on the right side of the face. Deceased's watch had stopped at 12.13. There was not the slightest sign of violence between the footpath and the river. A man needed to be careful going along this particular spot, even in the day time.

PC Williams gave evidence as to finding the body.

The jury returned a verdict of 'Accidentally drowned' and expressed their sympathy with the widow and relatives in their bereavement. They also added a rider to the verdict, to the effect that the place at present was exceedingly dangerous and that the people responsible should take some steps to have the fence put into a proper state of repair.

It seems it was a case of did he fall or was he pushed? He'd apparently had an altercation with someone in the Salmons and it is thought this person followed him an' did the dastardly deed ie pushed him in!

Of course, this meant that my mother and her brothers and sisters, twice daily, had to walk past the spot where he drowned – back and fore to school in Usk – which couldn't have been very pleasant for them.

Two of his sons, my mother's brothers, lost their lives in WWI - Uncle Will Parker and Uncle Dave Parker. Uncle Dave's body was never found and Uncle Will was killed by a sniper's bullet. He was apparently talking to his captain, saying, 'We gave the Hun a bashing this morning, sir,' when the sniper fired.

The small gold tin, pictured above, was given to troops in the First World War by Princess Mary as a present for their first Christmas in battle.[1] Overleaf is a short poem with a picture of the tin's contents:

Uncle Will - The Golden Tin

A gift from a Princess a small golden tin,
A few personal effects contained within,
A bullet, a medal, buttons a few,
Badges and keys once belonging to you.
What battles you fought, what hardships you
faced,
Your life in the trenches cannot be traced,
A sniper, one bullet your soul was released.

Scratched on the back of the tin, Private Parker deceased

My mother Winnie and her sister Lucy were placed 'in service' at Llancayo House *(opposite)* which was then owned by the Cowburns. However, the Cowburns soon moved from Llancayo House into Usk.

Because of this, my mother and her sister (my Auntie Lucy) were moved to other areas to complete their training. On leaving, they were given tokens, a show of appreciation, by the Cowburns. My mother was given a sewing/embroidery kit and my auntie was given a cross with a skull and crossbones on it *(opposite)*. She was told that this once belonged to the people who lived in the Windmill. These people, apparently 'Privateers' (legalised pirates),

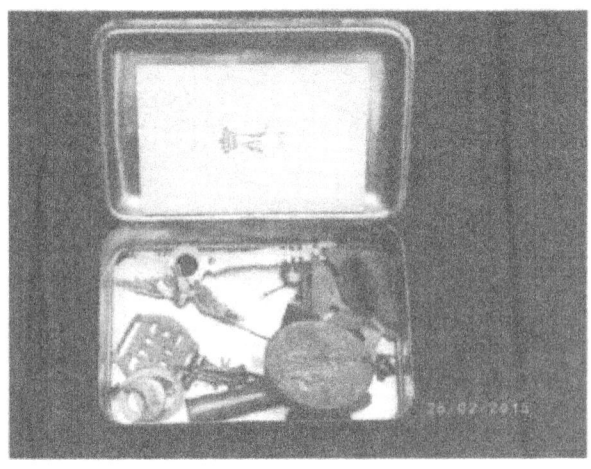

were given the Windmill at Llancayo as a thank you from a very grateful nation. The skull and crossbones on the cross would seem to fit in nicely with this story.[2]

We had plenty of extended family living close by. On my father's side, the Harrises, Uncle Ernest (Ern) Harris and his wife, Auntie Minnie, lived at Overbrook and Auntie Doll (Dorothy) and Uncle Aubrey lived at Walnut Tree Cottage – Auntie Doll was Dad's sister and married a Harris. Cyril Harris and Auntie Sis had lived at Hollow Farm in Gwehelog, about a mile away but had moved into Usk before my time.

On my mother's side, the Parker family, my Auntie Lucy married Ted Vaughan and lived at Llancayo. Teddy Parker and his wife May lived in Bettws Newydd – he was also a river warden.

These family members lived the nearest. Others lived in Usk - Uncle Ted lived in Mill Street in Usk and worked for Sweets the Builders - and Monmouth and some lived further afield in the Rhondda, Port Talbot and Cardiff.

I had two sisters, Doreen and Irene, both a lot older than me. Doreen was 21 when I was born, Irene 18. When Irene died, she was cremated and her ashes were scattered on The Common where she used to play when living at Overbrook.

Another sister, Lucy, died when she was six from appendicitis. I was just a baby when she died but apparently my name Graham came from the doctor/surgeon who was treating her. I never remember my older sisters living at home. They were both 'farmed out' to other family members who lived not too far away – Doreen to Aunty Lucy and Uncle Ted at Llancayo and Irene to Uncle Ern and Aunty Minnie at Overbrook Cottage, next to Trostrey Common - not only because of my arrival but also Gran Harris - my father's mother - who came to live with us, prior to me being born. The only recollection I have of Gran Harris is that she pinched my toast soldiers when I was having a boiled egg for breakfast! I vaguely remember being looked after by neighbours when she died. She is buried at Trostrey Church. After Gran Harris died, I had my own bedroom. Prior to that, I shared the bedroom with my parents.

I never knew or heard much about Grancha Harris, other than he died when my father was quite young.

My father worked on the Railway at Little Mill on shift work. He used to cycle to work – about seven miles - but later, he treated himself to a moped. He progressed to a BSA Bantam 125 a few years later - a great step up from the moped! He also did a spell at Pandy near Abergavenny, once again cycling to work – about 18 miles. Later, my father changed his job and got a new job with 'The Council' Roadworks department. This was much better as he was picked up by lorry at the bottom of Nyth House drive (our next-door neighbours).

Animals
We had a Welsh Springer spaniel, Rover, who was my best mate. When younger, we went everywhere together. We also had a budgie - Joey obviously! And before that, I can remember canaries.

Chapter 3 Home

I was born at Rose Cottage in Trostrey in January 1946 so I could be described as a baby boomer!

The original cottage comprised of just one room downstairs and two bedrooms upstairs with a fire grate in one. Flooring was flagstones and windows were sash and cord.

Rose Cottage in about 1990

There was no electricity. Lighting was provided by an 'Aladdin Lamp' which ran on paraffin. Ceilings were lath and plaster and the shadows cast by the lamp on the ceilings were a great source of entertainment. Shapes could be animals, birds or anything else that your imagination could take you when lying in bed – aaaah, such simple pleasures!

At one end of the downstairs room was the fireplace. At the other was a large table on which the majority of household chores were carried out. I would estimate the length and breadth of the room to be 20ft x 10ft.

The fire was cleaned every morning and ashes dumped on the garden and in deep ditches along the dirt track up on The

Rose Cottage in 2021

Top. In summertime, it was great relief not to have to do this but even then, the fire was lit in the evenings to boil water or kettles and for washing up. This was done in a bowl on the table but in the summer, the washing up bowl could be placed on the low wall outside. The dirty water was thrown over the garden or if there was a lot of it, tipped through the hedgerow on the other side of the lane which ran alongside the cottage.

To protect us from getting too close, the fireplace/grate was protected by a fender, an elaborate metal construction but lightweight and easily moved when the grate needed cleaning. Above the fire was the mantelpiece from which hung a small curtain with a drop of about 6 inches (health and safety were still very much in their infancy!). Above that was a mirror.

Either side of the fire were two alcoves. One held a grandfather clock (which I still have), the other was mostly for 'things which may be useful', plus carbide for cycle lamps. These were small lumps of chalky-like substance, grey in colour, which you put in your lamp, water was allowed to drip on it, which caused a reaction and produced the 'light'.

One wag on trips to the seaside thought it would be a good idea to take some carbide with him, then when he was on the

seashore, he would throw the carbide out to sea. The sea gulls, thinking it was food, would dive for it but as it hit the water, it would 'explode', causing great distress to the birds. Some found this amusing. I was not one of them!

We had a large garden which provided us with vegetables throughout the year. It also had apple and pear trees. My father was a great believer in growing his own veg throughout the various seasons, from Spring cabbage to purple sprouting and everything else in between, the last seasonal veg being swede. Fruit and veg were picked and stored in a large wooden shed (prior to this, in a small loft in the coalhouse) – formerly a chicken house. Although flowers were grown, these were solely for putting on graves at Trostrey church. My father's mantra was *'You can't eat blo*dy flowers!'* Flowers such as daffodils and spray chrysanths were grown in rows across the garden and were cut and put on the graves for special events, anniversaries. From a very early age, on one such visit, it was pointed out to me that bees nest in the Belfry at Trostrey Church and to this day, they still nest there.

Dad also rented about 15 acres of ground belonging to a Mr Evans who lived at Woodspring on the other lane. Because the area was higher up than the cottage, it was always known (by the family) as 'The Top'. A short walk up the narrow lane behind the cottage took you to 'The Top'.

The fields were banky, apart from one small paddock more or less directly behind the cottage, which was flat.

We eventually had a bin lorry but we had to take our rubbish down to the bottom of Nyth House drive for collection.

Chapter 4 Utilities

Tacked on the end of the cottage was the coal house, complete with a brick-built boiler tucked away in one corner. Coal was delivered by Eddie Cadogan from Usk and I still find it difficult to see how he managed to get the lorry (albeit a small one) with a ton of coal up the lane! Because there was nowhere to turn at Rose Cottage, we had to ask permission for Eddie to use Nyth House drive so that he could get to the bottom lane – there was never any problem with this.

The 'boiler' was situated in the corner of the coalhouse. This comprised of a rectangular stone and brick construction with a large metal tub fitted in the middle, under which was a small open fire. This was lit and kept going until the water was deemed hot enough to boil sheets and other whites'. The water was drawn from the large water tank. Drinking water was far too valuable to waste on washing. Ironing was done with a flat iron which was placed on the hob or hot top of the oven until deemed hot enough to iron the clothes.

The Tŷ Bach (or The Lav, as we called it!) was along a path, a good distance from the house! The contents of the bucket from the Tŷ Bach were emptied into a hole dug in the garden and yes, we did use cut or ripped up squares of newspapers as toilet paper.

Nearly all the cottages had their own well or like us shared a well, and obviously they had their own Tŷ Bach! Very few properties had their own flush toilets and bathrooms. The Council Houses at Llancayo were catered for in this way (then obviously, a new house at Tŷ Freeman Road, Gwehelog, many years later).

Electricity and water were put in sometime in the late 1950s. I can't remember which we had first.

In anticipation of this event, my father rebuilt the store shed and by knocking a doorway through, we gained an extra room, which became the kitchen. He also made the large single room into two, the idea being that this would be used as a dining area. A nice idea but rarely adhered to!

When my father replaced the store shed with what was to become 'the kitchen', the area had to be made bigger. This meant that barrow-loads of soil had to be shifted. This was 'barrowed' up the narrow track behind the cottage to the chicken run! My task was to pull the barrow with the aid of a rope whilst my father pushed it. I must admit, on occasions, not much pulling was done!

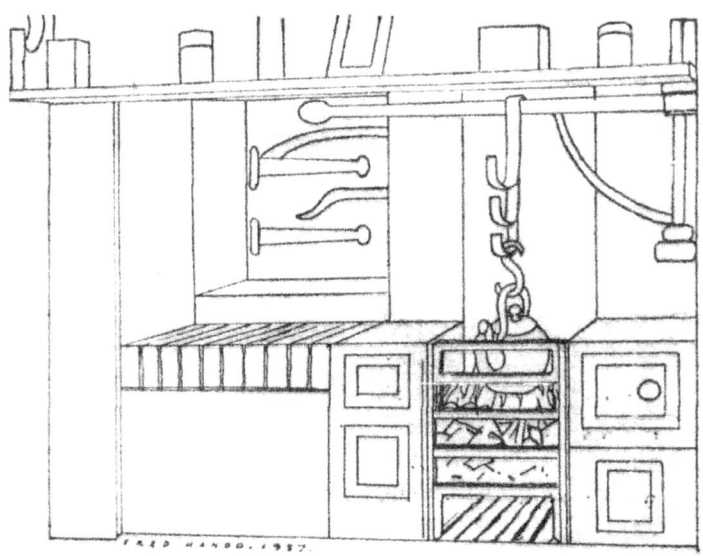

With this modernisation(!), we removed the old fire range and replaced it with a more modern fireplace/grate. At the back of the old range was a large hole which at some point had been used for making bread. When we looked closer, we found many of my old messages to Santa still intact but very brittle. The only thing we can think of is that some kind of draught must have blown them into this hole.

The Tŷ Bach we moved nearer to the cottage in place of the boiler in the coal house. We now became 'posh' because we had an Elsan bucket toilet and proper toilet paper.[1]

Although I must have been about 12 or 13, coming home from school, when I got to the top of the Chapel pitch – near Gwehelog Methodist Chapel – I could see our cottage on the hillside opposite and there was an outside light on, telling me that the electric was up and running. Once again, Mother claimed 'it wasn't nearly as good as the old Aladdin lamp!' Even so, having lights at, literally, the flick of a switch was, as my mother would say, 'a Godsend'. To have a light in your bedroom rather than the small candlelight lamp flickering away was great and meant I could actually read in bed.

We eventually invested in a small fridge and tumble drier, electric iron, plus an electric cooker/oven, and an electric kettle, also a variety of electric tools. Now we had a fridge, milk could be stored therein.

Before running water arrived, a large tank at the end of the coalhouse caught rainwater (soft) which was used for washing clothes and to fill up the tin bathtub when needed!

Water was also stored in a huge tank on the property of Claude Cornfield, Wainfield Lane. This tank was visible for miles around and must have been 50plus feet above the skyline. It stored enough water to supply all the cottages in Gwehelog and Trostrey. It's not so very long ago that the tank was dismantled, and water was piped, I believe, from the pumping station in Usk near The Rhadyr. I can only assume the water to fill the tank originally came from Llandegfedd.[2]

We now had water on tap. However, there wasn't anywhere to run the water away so a bucket was put under the sink (in the new kitchen) and then emptied, either down the lane or into a nearby unused garden or the field on the other side of the lane. No bathing or toilet facilities were incorporated in the new or existing cottage. The tin bath was still in use, but my sister and brother-in-law had moved into the Council Houses at Gwehelog (opposite Hall Inn pub) so we used to pop over there for a bath, sheer luxury! For normal everyday living, we still relied on a quick swill and strip wash.

Although a certain amount of clothes washing was still done by hand, my sister Doreen in the Council House would do the 'big washing' and ironing, so life was becoming a bit easier for my Mother. I must admit it was a bit sad to see the large old mangle machine, always outside the new back door, being carted away for scrap.

Conclusion – It sounds a very hard life but it was all we knew and just got on with it. But having water and electric installed certainly made things a lot easier.

Chapter 5 Usk

Most shopping, apart from what was delivered to us, was done in Usk. I can still remember most of the shops and it's fascinating to see how they've changed over the decades. I'll start at Twyn Square and work my way down through Bridge Street to the Bridge.

The clock, now forming a roundabout in the centre of Twyn Square, was then situated on the corner of the Square in front of the Church/Chapel. It was moved from there to where the other end of the Square, before being moved again to its present location in the centre.[1]

Shops on the Square included Harold Knowles' fish and chip shop, Gibbons, a small grocery general store, Harry Savery's car work shop, the Nag's Head pub,[2] then the Bank[3] on the corner which also contained other offices. On the Old Chepstow Road going out of the Square was the Greyhound pub,[4] then the Olway, also a pub.[5]

On the other side of the Square, approximately opposite Gibbons, was Perry's bakery and the Castle pub.[6] Where the small carpark is now, there used to be a row of houses and a café on the corner, behind which was part of Sweets (the builders) works yard. Hughes Brothers were also builders. I believe they had a yard near the Olway.

Returning to the main street, and turning right out of the Square, up the Monmouth road for a few yards, you had Windows café (nicknamed Stinkers by the locals) and opposite was Ted the Box funeral directors and home for his funeral parlour.

Back past Twyn Square, there was Clenches garage and shops, then the bank - Barclays?[7] Opposite Clenches was a small hairdressers. On the corner of the Abergavenny road was Frank Hobbs general store - Excel Stores - next to which was the Corn Stores which sold animal foodstuffs. Further along the Abergavenny road was Sweets fishing tackle shop. On the corner where Abergavenny Road and Bridge Street meet was the Three Salmons Hotel.[8] Opposite on the corner of Maryport Street and Bridge Street was the White Hart pub.[9] Following on that side of the street was Walters, a small jewellery shop, next to which was Midgeleys sweet shop. Mr and Mrs Midgeley were 'Actors' and really played the part of retired thespians. They were both colourful characters. He always wore plus fours. I blame them for my addiction to chocolate! I believe next there was a fruit and veg shop called Charles's and a bit further down was Morgan and Davies' shoe shop, a Co-op and then Stan Weare's, the tobacconist and barbers. That was a magical place to go into with all the smells of tobacco, snuff and shaving soap and cream. Stan employed Mr Weston who also cut hair. There was also another barber called Bill Hickey but I never went there. Morleys, the wool shop, came next, then Hendersons, the paper shop, followed by Cozens, the bakers, next to which was the butcher's shop Pitts, which became Harleys who delivered our meat. There was also Mullins and Haggets (?), also a butchers, before Bowyers who sold fresh fruit and veg, as well as fish. I believe it was the Rendezvous café next.

Sheddicks was another shop at this end of town. They did cycle repairs and parts, plus I believe motor cycle parts. Near Sheddicks was the Old Jew Shop - I know in today's climate this is not very pc but that is what it was known as. Whether it was called that because it was owned/run by an elderly Jewish gentleman or maybe it was just a very old shop, I have no idea. The lady who worked there fascinated me because she had the hairiest chin I have ever seen! The shop sold bric–a-brac (posh name for junk shop) Tom Lewis' grocers was the next one along, then the Golden Lion pub.[10] A bit further another bank, then came the chemist with a paper shop/newsagents next door. Next to them was a small shop called Athertons who also sold fruit and veg. Bunnings was a hardware store and builders merchants, and finally the Cardiff Arms pub.[11]

Turning left onto New Market Street, opposite was the police station, then a bit further down was Lathams, the butchers, then the surgery. I remember Dr Bird and Dr Horton were resident doctors. Then on the corner was the

Royal British Legion, opposite which was a small sweet shop. On the other side of the building between Mill Street and Baron Street was Nelmes' grocery shop. The Royal pub[12] was owned by the Jones family - Ted the Box funeral directors - and other members of the family ran the pub. In the yard at the back was the workshop for coffin making. On the corner of Old Market Street was the King's Head pub.[13]

Returning to Bridge Street and heading from the Town Bridge back to Twyn Square, Vin Jones' grocers which used the old system that, if you paid for your goods by a note of any denomination, it was clipped to a wire and sent to an office which appeared to be suspended in mid-air further in the shop. This was manned by an assistant whose job it was to unclip the note and secure it in a till. Next came the Post Office, followed by the Cross Keys pub,[14] then a shoe shop Morgans and then Hathaways, a small general store. There was another shop between Hathaways and Smiths, the drapers, but I can't for the life of me remember what it was or what it sold. Smiths was a very large drapers shop. My Aunty Lucy from Llancayo worked there and used to cycle from home on an old fashioned 'sit up and beg' bike in all winds and weathers. This shop was later bought by a Mr Churnside who diversified by breeding Chinchillas in the basement/cellar. Lastly on this side came Thomas the bike shop who did cycle repairs and sold bicycle parts and equipment.

Maryport Street had a bookies, a few doors down from the White Hart. Next was a hairdressers - Rees' (Rosemary) - then the Conservative Club, then the Secondary School. Opposite the school was Hickeys, a small grocers and sweet shop, which basically was the school's tuck shop. They had row after row of the large old fashioned sweet jars, from which you could buy 4ozs of anything, which Nelly (Hickey) would weigh and bag up for you. There were two schools along Maryport Street, the boys' and girls' school – separate, of course. The Gatehouse for the Priory was more or less opposite the Lamb and Flag,[15] then the New Court Inn,[16] the Sessions House[17] and the Memorial Hall.[18]

Opposite this was the Borstal.[19] The Borstal boys were allowed out around the town to do a variety of jobs. They wore a grey uniform and rode bicycles around the town and out to Cefn Ila, a sort of open prison which stood next to the maternity hospital. At the end of the street was the Cricket Grounds and Clubhouse. The Borstal playing fields were next to the cricket field and they had their own clubhouse

.

Chapter 6 Food

We were basically self-sufficient but still needed some groceries such as sugar, tea, bread and flour, plus other supplies which we couldn't make or grow for ourselves. It's funny how life sometimes overlaps. A good many years ago now (about 50), I remember Frank Hobbs (Excel Stores Usk) delivering our groceries on a Friday evening. He explained to my father that the bread was the last free bread (a yearly event) allocated to 'The Poor of the Parish' because the money had run out. I'm not sure where the money came from for this donation but I have the feeling whoever the donor was, was from a military background.

Not long after Jill and I moved into our present home at Canal Cottage in Llanellen, a gentleman came around. He was researching his family history and explained that Canal Cottage was known as 'A Friendly House'. Near the cottage was a post with three marks carved in it. These marks indicated that if people from the Workhouse (in Abergavenny) were walking by, they could call in and have a free meal of bread.

There were four grocers delivering in those days – Vin Jones, Cledwynn Lewis, Frank Hobbs and the 'Midnight Baker' (from Llangwm). I didn't know him but he got his name from the fact he delivered groceries very late in the evening!

Our bread came from Cozens bakery whose bread was the best anywhere around, especially their cob. If I had to go to Usk for shopping, it was the last place we called at to buy a cob. We asked them to wrap it up well because we either had to catch the bus home (getting off at Cold Harbour, about a mile from Rose Cottage) or cycled home via Llancayo. By the time we arrived home, it was still warm and was eaten straight away with lashing of home-made butter spread over it. I have never tasted better bread and butter.

At the top of the garden was the chicken run. There was also a pigsty. At the back of the house was another shed which held animal food/feedstuffs and tools etc.

My father kept store cattle, usually about half a dozen, and a milking cow, a Jersey cow called 'The Old Girl'. I mention this because if I refer to 'the old girl' further along this tale, you will know who I am referring to!

'The Old Girl' was still young enough to produce calves. To take her to the bull meant half a day's work. We literally led her via the lanes and tracks to The Hill Farm, about a mile away where the bull was ready and waiting. Obviously, the Old Girl insisted on munching her way along the lanes so it was a slow old process to get there. Once there, she was 'put to the bull' which left myself and Father free to chat or wander around. I was often lifted up on to the working horses - cart horses. They were monsters! I had to sit on them sideways because my little legs were too short to straddle their backs! We were invited in for a cuppa. I remember the 'parlour' being a large area and the floor covered in mosaic/marble tiles. Apparently, a group of Italian artisans travelled around the country not long after WWII, doing this mosaic/marble tiling work. There was also a grand piano in there. Whether any of family ever played or not, I don't know.

Once the bull had completed his duty, we walked The Old Girl back home. I'm sure she had a spring in her step as we meandered along lanes and tracks. I helped deliver the calf (heifer, in this instance) after about ten months.

For the next calf, I'm afraid The Old Girl didn't have the pleasure of meeting the bull because the AI man saved him (the bull) the trouble! AI - Artificial Insemination.

Sadly, we had to get rid of the Old Girl and half a dozen store cattle. They contracted bovine TB. She had been part of 'the family' for about ten years.

This next passage is gory and barbaric. Seriously, I think you should consider this before going on but I would ask you to try to understand it was how things were done at that time. Please remember these events took place over 60 years ago.

My Auntie Lucy told us kids about the abattoir on the riverbank near the weir. Apparently, the river ran red with blood from the slaughtering. A bit gory but part of the rich tapestry, I suppose.

At home, chickens were killed by putting a narrow-bladed, extremely sharp knife down their throats, allowing them to bleed to death. They were held by their legs and swung back and forth until they stopped bleeding and fluttering.

Once this had been achieved, the hen was plucked and giblets removed. Sometimes these would be used to create a stock for other meals. My mother did the plucking and used to help local chicken farmers at Christmas time when pluckers were in big demand. She was very adept at this task. (Their method for despatching 'birds' was very much more humane).

Stuffing was usually parsley and thyme. Thyme was picked from off the Common at the bottom of the lane. Now no longer growing there, it was outcompeted by more pernicious weeds and trees, many years ago.

When the pig(s) were ready for slaughter, the local farmer, Walter Jenkins, would come over with his 4.10 (four-ten) hand gun and shoot them. The pig was brought down from the sty and stood in the lane. Walter would then place the gun against her forehead and despatch her. Death was almost instant. She would collapse, twitch for a moment or two, then lie quiet. After a short while, she was slit from her chin to her tail and allowed to bleed. To say the lane was red with blood is no exaggeration. We were given the bladder to play with, which was the size of the average balloon.[1] I'm not sure how Walter was paid, possibly by having a few prime cuts from the pig.

When ready, the pig was carried to the coalhouse and placed on a very strong wooden table. It was then cut into 'flitches'. These were hung on the coalhouse wall, covered in muslin until ready to be jointed up. The head was used to make brawn. We were told that you could eat all of the pig *'from its grunt to its tail'*. The innards, those which could be used, were used to make faggots and the large intestine – chitlings - was also seen as some sort of delicacy. Chitlings had to be thoroughly washed, preferably with running water. The pig's brains were my father's choice!

To supplement our diet, we caught rabbits, shot pheasants and pigeons, and caught the odd trout or two and eels from the nearby brook. Rabbits were caught either by ferreting – I used to go with my Uncle Aubrey – or snares (wires in our day). Rabbits were skinned and paunched almost immediately. This task was easier to do when they were still warm.

At first, our milk came from 'The Old Girl' but after we had to get rid of her, we had to find a new supply of milk. As luck would have it, the neighbours living at Arosfa (the two Miss Rogers, sisters) had a milking cow so they were our suppliers until they sold up and moved to The Glade.

Our next supplier was the people at the Dyffrin who also kept wild fowl. We called them Galenies(?). They had a distinctive call which sounded like 'go back go back' and they used to roost in trees. Eventually the people moved from the Dyffrin. By then, we had a milkman - Claude Cornfield from Wainfield Lane, Gwehelog. When he retired, Ralph Lewis from Tŷ-Freeman Road took over and was our milkman for many years.

Day to day living was basically divided between mealtimes – breakfast, dinner, tea and supper and more or less had fixed times. These did vary at differing times of the year and season. Other than bread, most meals were 'home grown' and consisted of seasonal veg and when available, home-produced chicken and pig/bacon, although beef was a typical Sunday roast, as was lamb when in season. When we stopped producing our own meat, we had meat delivered by the butchers - Ern Harley, then Courtney from Bridge Street in Usk.

Before we had the new kitchen, cooking was done on a very old-fashioned range with two ovens, one for slow cooking and t'other for normal cooking. There was also a hob for kettles and suchlike but saucepans (more than one) were balanced precariously on a ring/s just above the open fire.

My mother was great at baking, much of which she learned whilst 'in Service'. Cakes were always available, as was a cup of tea! I still remember the taste of the cake mix. We were allowed to run our fingers around the large bowl to collect the remains left there, after the mix had been put in the oven. I believe the large bowl is now described as 'Creamware', being pale yellow and patterned on the outside.

Postmen, delivery boys and anyone else passing or working nearby were invited in to sample cakes, tarts (we had tarts in those days, not pies) all home-made, as were jams, pickles and sauces. If we ran out of anything, we could always pop over to Thomas The Shop, a small shop which catered for the local community. It's now a house.

A cheese press was used in the making of cheese. When the cheese was fit to eat, one of my Father's favourites was Welsh rarebit and I remember him making toast in front of the open fire, then on the special long-handled fork he had made, a slice of cheese was held over the toast and the cheese allowed to drip onto it, toast and cheese never tasted better.

This wasn't sliced bread, slices were cut from a loaf which I'm sure was named a 'Tin loaf'.

We also had steamed apples or baked apples. These were covered in suet. For steaming, muslin was used to wrap the apples in. Muslin seemed to be used for just about everything from making cheese to all sorts of culinary delights.

Chapter 7 Clothing

We had a 'tally man', a Mr Hicks from Pontypool, who supplied us with clothes - shirts, trousers, bloomers for Mother, long johns for Father, jackets, suits, some made to measure.[1] There were also two 'hawkers' who used to catch the bus to Cold Harbour, then tout their large cases to all the cottages. One was an old lady who apparently was part of the Danters Dynasty, who were Fairground travellers based in Chepstow.[2] Another was a Sikh gentleman who sold mostly cosmetics. We didn't see many turban wearers in Trostrey so he was a bit of a distraction! It must have been a hard life, carrying heavy cases around with you all day, but it obviously paid.

Mending and darning were major chores! Collars, when worn on the inside, were turned so that the worn/frayed areas were now on the outside at the bottom of the collar and so could not be seen as your jacket or coat covered this area. Of course, Robin starch was used to stiffen the collar.

Equally, sheets, if getting a bit thin in the middle, were cut and stitched in a certain way so the thin areas were now on the edge of the sheet and could be tucked under the mattress. And there were always socks to be darned! Darning and stitching were evening 'pastimes' and done under the glow of the Aladdin lamp. Very little material was wasted. Any old clothes were kept for 'patching'.

You had your 'good clothes' for going out and you had your work clothes. My father always wore a flat cap, quite often indoors! Granddad shirts , braces, turnups on trousers, hand knitted cardigans/waistcoats, long johns, stockings (not tights!) and of course a bowler hat and black tie for funerals and black shoe/boot polish were also essential!

Shirts had detached collars for which you needed a stud to fit them in place. A stud box was a necessity and was stored on the top shelf of a large cupboard along with shaving equipment.

Shoes, if beginning to wear out, were heeled and soled by kits you could buy. The worn shoe was placed on the 'last' and soles and heels were tacked onto the shoe. This was much cheaper than buying a new pair every time they became a bit worn. A last was a metal foot-shaped plate fitted on a block of wood about a yard in length. Shoes to be repaired were placed over the metal plate and the new soles and/or heels (sometimes both) were tacked onto the shoe. The fact it was on a block of wood meant you didn't have to bend too much to do this repair job, as you could hold it between your knees.

My mother, for special occasions, would cram herself into a 'corset' (sometimes called 'stays'). This was a tight-fitting pink affair, hour glass in shape (similar to a basque) with whalebone strips fitted around the sides and back. The back was laced up as tight as could be, thus holding in any surplus flesh, and clips hung down to affix stockings to. I'm sure this was all very uncomfortable but with the corset worn under her new frock, my Mother seemed very pleased with the end result. I remember her complaining when they replaced whalebone with plastic strip that these didn't 'hold her in' like the whalebone did in her old corsets.

My father used a 'cut throat razor' which was sharpened on a long leather strop hung on the back of a door. I did try the cut-throat razor but only a few times. Well, there's only so much blood you can lose.

Later, he had a more modern version. This (as far as I remember) comprised of a small(ish) tin, approximately 6 inches by 4 inches. The razor and small strop were enclosed and you ran the razor backwards and forwards along the strop until sharp.

Walter Jenkins, a local farmer who killed our pigs, also used to cut hair – short, back and sides which cost about 2/- for adults and 1/6d for me. He was also d*mn good at cutting hedges, especially with a long-handled hook, (a very skilled operation). Obviously, he transferred his hedge cutting skills to a pair of scissors!

Before we discovered Walter, my father used to take me to Stan's in Usk to have my hair cut. Transport was a push bike. I had my own little saddle with stirrups which could be clipped on to the crossbar of the bike so I could hold on to the handlebars. I really thought I was Roy Rogers on Trigger!

Haircuts in those days were short back and sides. But then 'a square neck haircut' became the fashion which came just after the Teddy boy style - bouffant front and a DA at the back (to put it mildly, DA stood for the nether regions of a duck)[3]. When this fashion came in, I went to Stans and asked for a square neck haircut but he was quite reluctant to do it, asking 'if I had had permission from my father for this style of cut.'

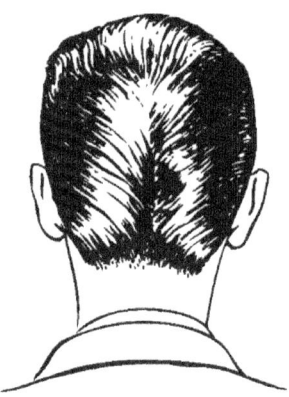

And Mother had to have a 'perm' if going somewhere special. I can still smell the perm fixer(?) to this day.

Strip washing kept us clean, although I did have my own special small tin bath which had to be emptied by bucket because it was too heavy to lift and carry outside. Bathing was done in front of the fire. We did have the usual large tin bath which on occasions was used. Once again, the problem was emptying it. Mostly, it was a quick swill of face and hands, then strip wash the rest. Our necks and behind our ears were always checked to make sure we had 'swilled ' them properly.

Chapter 8 Chores

From quite an early age, we had to help with various chores, for example collecting morning wood, carry water, help with the cattle, milk the cow and use the milk churn These 'chores' seemed quite enjoyable and I don't remember being hard done by or put upon. We did what we had to do, then went out to play.

Drinking water was carried from 'The Well', approximately 500 yards down the lane. I had my own special tin jug (which held a gallon) for carrying water. It was almost a rite of passage to be able to carry the jug - from The Well to home - without putting it down for a rest. You really felt 'grown up' then!

We were shown which wood to collect for the fire. Some wood(s) are better than others for starting or lighting fires.

The Firewood Poem

Beechwood fires are bright and clear
If the logs are kept a year,
Chestnuts only good they say,
If for logs 'tis laid away.
Make a fire of elder tree,
Death within your house will be;
But ash new or ash old,
Is fit for a queen with crown of gold.

Birch and fir logs burn too fast,
Blaze up bright and do not last.
It is by the Irish said
Hawthorne bakes the sweetest bread.
Elm wood burns like a churchyard mould,
Even the very flames are cold.
But ash green or ash brown
Is fit for a queen with golden crown.

Poplar gives a bitter smoke,
Fills your eyes and makes you choke.
Apple wood will scent your room,
Pear wood smells like flowers in bloom.
Oaken logs, if dry and old,
Keep away the winter's cold,
But ash wet or ash dry
A king shall warm his slippers by.
(Lady Celia Congreve 1930)

The cowshed was cleaned/cleared out by pitchfork and wheelbarrow. We had a dung heap, but during the autumn and winter months, the dung was 'barrowed' straight onto the fields which was damned hard work but kept you warm! My father made me my own little wheelbarrow but as I grew older, my 'expertise' was transferred to the big barrow (which he also built himself).

Milking the cow was also a skill. You had to squeeze the teat in a certain way and gently slide your fingers down the length of the teat to get the optimum milk. We used to get at least a bucket full. We weren't allowed to carry it from 'The 'Top' down to the cottage in case we spilt it! Milk had to be bottled, then stood in water in the summer or thundery weather to stop it 'going off'. The bucket was placed in the coolest place and/or in the shade.

The milk was used for tea obviously, and for making milk puddings and butter. As children, we used to love using the churn to make the butter, turning and turning until my mother looked at it and felt it was ready to make butter. We still had the little wooden pat-a-cake paddles until a few years ago. Home-made butter was the best I have ever tasted although, by today's standards, it would be deemed too salty. I remember my mother complaining that 'You couldn't get Rennet anymore'.[1] This came in a small stone jar approximately 6inches tall (yes, we used inches in those days!). It was off-white with a cork stopper and was used for 'setting' stuff, I believe for butter and jam or anything else that needed to be 'set'.

Chapter 9 Play and Friends

Despite the chores, we still had plenty of time to play and make mischief! I and a few pals were allowed to roam around the woods, fields and any derelict cottages, streams, climb trees and go 'birdnesting', collecting eggs (we were only allowed to take one to add to our collection). We had the freedom to do more or less what we wanted, go where we wanted without fear (other than falling in a brook or out of a tree!). There didn't seem to be any pressure. We made up our own fun, there wasn't the 'organised happiness' we see today. There was always someone around with whom we could share our joy, excitement, tears, sadness, be they family friends or neighbours. There were always bows and arrows to make, catapults, neighbours to wind up, scrumping apples, or any edible fruit for that matter, building dens. We always seemed to have plenty to do so there was no time to become bored or fed up and we seemed to cope with tragedy without too much fuss. There was always a bedtime story when we eventually went to bed, Rupert Bear being a firm favourite. We loved anything by Mabel Lucy Atwell who also produced calendars, mostly, as far as I can remember with babies or very young children on.[1]

As youngsters, we were always looking for somewhere to make a 'Den'. Although the driveway from Nyth House was private (apart from the top section which has a registered footpath status), there were some magnificent oaks growing alongside the drive. One in particular made an ideal 'tree den'. Of course, no one could see us when we were playing or hiding in there.

We used to have great fun annoying the farmer next door to the Nyth by hiding and yelling at him as he tried to get the cattle in for milking. Our performance frightened them so he and his wife had to chase them until they eventually went in! He was from the Valleys (his name was Harris too but no connection to us) but he was nicknamed 'Old Butt Harris',

43

because, as he came from the Valleys, he called everyone Butt or Butty. He married Nellie, a local spinster.

Along the ridge from Camp Wood (belonging to Usk Castle), there is another woodland which stretches nearly into Usk. We discovered two underground shelters *(see map overleaf and pictures on following page – these belong to the Humphreys of Usk Castle)* built in woodland next and near to the small forestry area - one at the top of the wood and one at the bottom - approximately in line with each other. We were told these were constructed during the Second World War to store goods and materials and possibly members of the auxiliary unit Esau (Usk) which comprised of local residents who would act as a militia force if we were invaded by the Germans.[2]

A few years ago, I took local naturalist Colin Titcombe to these shelters as part of his research into the Esau Auxiliary Unit (Usk), We managed to clamber down a large branch into the shelters and discovered that they were now home to cave spiders (*Meta menardi*) and bats (Lesser Horseshoe bat *(Rhinolophus hipposideros)* and the remains of dead animals eg foxes, badgers and sheep.

And of course, when we were older, we had bikes. My first bike was purchased from the Tranters at the Dyffrin. It was a child's bike, black in colour. My Auntie Lucy bought me a new bike when I was about 13 or 14. This was a racing bike with drop handlebars and a deraileur for changing gears.[3] My nearby neighbours, the Jones's (John and Alan), had a trike but I could never get on with this. I wanted to tip it up on to two wheels!

We also had comics *Beano*[4] and *Dandy*[5] and occasionally we'd go 'upmarket' and buy *The Eagle*.[6] Annuals of these were always put on our Christmas lists, along with cowboy and/or Indian suits, marbles and a Dinky toy or two. [7]

Our comics and books came from Hendersons in Usk. I remember, I was about 15, buying the DH Lawrence book, *Lady Chatterley's Lover*.[8] Pip Dean was the shop assistant – a rather large, stern-looking lady – who, when I handed over the book, started tutting. Glaring at me, she put it in a brown

paper bag and literally threw it onto the counter for me to pick up. I swear she then went and washed her hands! Pip used to live at the cottage at Cold Harbour and on many occasions, we caught the same bus to go into Usk. She used to still glare at me and shake her head.

The only time I can remember being slightly peeved about living in the countryside was when roller skates became the 'in thing'. On our lanes and roads, they were a no no. We also played with 'bowlys', *(see page 48)* metal hoops or bicycle wheels' which we would bowl along the lanes and run after. My father used to talk about the miles he and his friends would travel around the lanes, driving and wheeling this hoop with a piece of stick. Once again, simple pleasures.

Sunday visits by members of the family were a regular occurrence. Children in those days were not allowed to be part of, or within hearing distance, of adult conversation, so, while they all chatted, myself and cousins would take an air gun and shoot rats which were pretty plentiful around the chicken run and coop We also had a 'rat gun', a single-shot cartridge gun which had a range of no more that 30ft. A 03,

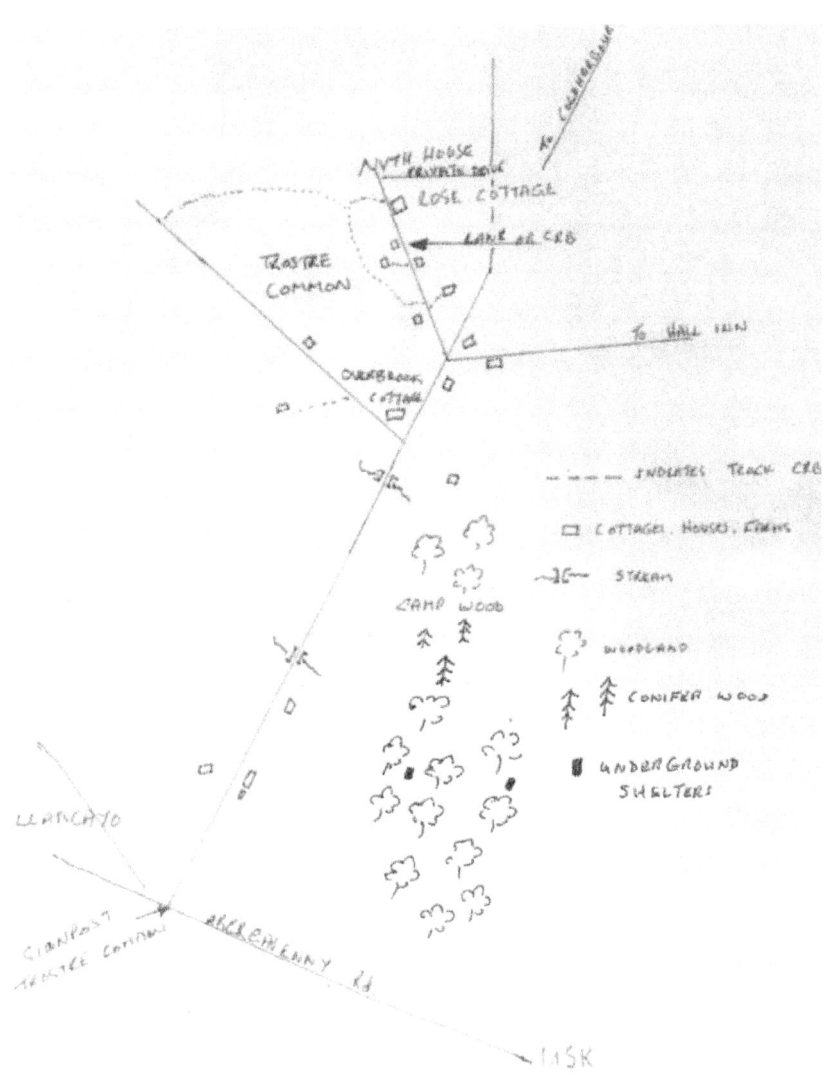

NTH HOUSE
PRIVATE DRIVE
ROSE COTTAGE

TO CWMBRAS...

LANE OR CRB

TRASTRE COMMON

TO HALL INN

OVERBROOK COTTAGE

CAMP WOOD

-- -- -- INDICATES TRACK CRB

☐ COTTAGES, HOUSES, FARMS

)≡(STREAM

WOODLAND

CONIFER WOOD

UNDERGROUND SHELTERS

LLANGATO

SIGNPOST
TRASTRE COMMON

ABERGAVENNY RD

USK

I believe, (no, definitely not 303!) 4.10 was usually a shotgun less powerful than the customary 12 bore. To make a bit more pocket money, we used to shoot grey squirrels, mostly with air guns. If we took the tail to George Hathaway's shop in Bridge Street in Usk, he would give us 10 shillings per tail (about £13 in today's money).

Opposite Rose Cottage was an orchard so I really didn't have far to go to scrump apples! One variety I remember was Tom Putt, a blotched red medium-sized apple. I'm not sure now if this was an eater or cooker or it may have been dual purpose. We had our own apple tree, a dual purpose one. I believe it was called 'Underleaf', a green apple. Every autumn, I had to pick these and we put them into storage in the shed. I must admit I hated the job. Even when I had children of my own, every autumn half term up to Rose Cottage we would go for me to pick apples! After I sold Rose Cottage, a few years ago, the people who eventually bought it and modernised it, cut down this apple tree to build a garage. I must admit I did have a few pangs of sadness to see it gone, despite hating the annual job of picking its apples!

Most cottages had orchards, many growing cider apples or perry pears which were sold to breweries such as Bulmers.[9] To supplement our pocket money, we used to pick apples and pears for the cottages with orchards.

Also, we used to go to farms and hoe between rows of swedes or whatever, and go spud picking.

We knew where to find watercress, (pwllcaes, pool field, on Russel Hill Farm), the best fields for mushrooms, (the fields behind Nyth House), best woods for chestnuts, (New Wood, Hill Farm) and conker trees, cherry trees and elderflower/berry bushes, as well as wild plums (Bullace), both blue and yellow varieties.

The mother of a school friend of mine (David Williams) worked as a cook for Lord Raglan at Cefn Tilla Court.[10] I went over to play with David and met his Lordship who took us to a small room in which he kept trays and trays of birds' eggs. Whether he had collected them himself or had bought them, I don't know but it made our meagre collections seem very inadequate.

We had seasonal favourites too. In the spring, we would eat the young shoots and leaves of hawthorn. It was known as 'bread and cheese' (though I have no idea why!). There were also ground or pignuts to be dug up.[11] These had a slightly peppery taste but were lovely.

When we had visitors on a Sunday in the autumn, if the weather was kind, we would all go out nut picking. There would probably be half a dozen or so of us. We would take a blanket which was put on the ground under the nut tree. It was the job of us kids to climb or shake the tree so that nuts fell on the blanket. This made it much easier to pick them up, rather than raking around in the grass or whatever.

Bonfire night was a fairly quiet affair with a few rockets, bangers, Catherine wheels and of course, sparklers. You could buy a mixed box of fireworks for 12/6d. I usually built a small fire. My sister and brother-in-law came over with a few extra fireworks.

At Christmas time, we cut holly and mistletoe, took it up to Cold Harbour and sold it to passing motorists, all so that we could have a bit extra to spend in the tuck shop - Hickeys (One Stop Shop now) - opposite the old Secondary School. Nellie Hickey was more than happy to supply us with any sweets and drinks we could afford.

Also at Christmas, a gang of us went carol singing. During the evening, we visited most of the cottages around, walking miles in the dark. Sometimes one of us would remember to take a torch!

Once a year, a crowd of us would mow the churchyard at Trostrey. This was done by hand with hooks (sickles) and scythes. The unused area was done with the scythe but around the graves and headstones, we used the hook. The actual graves themselves were cut with hand shears on a regular basis.

When older, a gang of us boys and sometimes girls used to meet at Cold Harbour. This was roughly a halfway point between us and Llandenny. We usually congregated there on our bikes and used to have competitions to see who could do the most tricks on them.

On a very sad note, when I was about 6 or 7, myself and two chums were fed up with the words of the Lord's Prayer so we changed some of the words for 'bucket'. I've no idea why. For example, *The Lord is my bucket .... He maketh me to lie down in green buckets...* We giggled hysterically and had great fun! Sadly, next day Inigo (Matthews - his mother was German) was knocked over by a vehicle and died. It was not sure what exactly happened. Some say he stepped out from behind a bus opposite the Council school and was hit by a car. Others say he was hit by the bus. I remember Arthur Knowles, the postman, picked him up and tried to save him, sadly to no avail. At his funeral, we took small bunches of flowers, posies to throw on the grave. I don't remember any of us being traumatised that he had died and gone to Heaven which, as we all knew then, was a wonderful place and still is to children today, no doubt.

When in 'big school', a pal of ours committed suicide. We never found out why. Another pal was killed when the motorbike his friend was driving crashed in New Barn Bends in Gwehelog. We seemed to accept, even at such young ages, that tragedies occurred and it was all part of growing up. If we were upset, we had parents, family to turn to and mates who would console us and try to ease our pain. Looking back, we did seem to be more practical about life and death but also having the wherewithal to enjoy life to the full and really appreciate the good times.

All in all, by today's standard, I would call it idyllic.

Chapter 10 Entertainment

At home, the wireless was our main source of entertainment. Ours was quite a bulky thing which stood on the windowsill. On many occasions, I had to ride my bike into Usk to buy a 'battery' for the wireless. This consisted of a rather large, pale blue square jar filled with weird-looking small square objects which we had to be careful not to spill because they contained acid.

Radio then had three programmes – the Light Programme which had lighter comedy and music, the Home Service which catered for drama and serious stuff, and the Third which was classical music. On the Light Programme, Anne Shelton *(below)* was a big hit, especially with the troops and their families.[1]

One song I can remember went something like this:
Come to the station, Jump from the train,
March at the double, Down lover's lane.
Then in the glen where the roses entwine,
Lay down your arms and surrender to mine ...

They don't write love songs like that anymore! And who could forget *How Much is That Doggy in the Window, the one with the waggily tail woof woof?*[2] This was a great favourite on bus trips - Sunday school and such like. Of course, everyone joined in on the *woof woof* bit!

For us children, there was always Uncle Mac on a Saturday morning.[3] This was not to be missed. I still remember *A Four-Legged Friend* which was sung by cowboy Roy Rogers, never thinking that in 60 years' time, I'd be looking after five of them! (horses, plus a feral goat).[4]

Mostly, we listened to The Home Service but on a Sunday, we listened to The Light Programme, especially *Family Favourites* which catered mostly for BFPO - troops who were stationed mostly abroad.[5] BFPO – British Forces Post Office. Their families could send in requests for records to be played for them - a two-way process.

This was usually followed by *Life with the Lyons,* an early soap opera.[6] Later on, we could listen to the Top 40. The Home Service catered for more serious listening. I was very jealous of the Jones family, at Lower House (Alan, John and Irene), as their father Bill allowed them to listen to Radio Luxembourg which mostly played pop music.

I was about 15 when we had our first television - black and white obviously. Previously I visited neighbours who already had a telly if there was something important on, which wasn't very often! I did visit Mr Bill Powell, his wife Kit and their two daughters Anne and Pat (Judith, their third daughter, came along later) at Cherry Tree Cottage to watch a programme about Louis Pasteur.

Favourite shows on the 'new telly' were *Bootsie and Snudge*[7] and *Sunday Night at the London Palladium.*[8] We enjoyed Dave King[9] who was a comedian and Hughie Green[10] who hosted a quiz programme called *Double Your Money.*[11] And I watched the first episode of *Coronation Street* which made me late for youth club!

Cousin Nancy was treated to a gramophone which, as far as I remember, was a wind-up one and you had to change the needle fairly often, otherwise it would scratch. The pop idol of the day was an American Paul Anka but I can't remember what he sang.[12]

We also had home entertainment - board games such as Ludo, Snakes and Ladders, Housey Housey (Bingo), Snap, Happy Families and, as mentioned elsewhere, a singalong on a Saturday night.

Growing up in Usk as a youngster could sometimes be a bit limiting so there was the opportunity improvise!

When young, we were taken to the pictures in Usk - The Red Shed which is actually green. I remember seeing a film there called *The Greatest Show on Earth* which I found very sad because the hero died (I think) but it was explained that he hadn't really died and he would, in all probability, be in the next film.[13] One very old lady always shone her light on the film and kept muttering to it, which was a great source of enjoyment.

Red Shed Saturday mornings were good – The Bowery Boys,[14] Roy Rogers and obviously Chaplin.[15] If you sat at the back in front of the projector, you could do all sorts of weird and wonderful things with your hands and fingers which would be relayed onto the screen. For example, you could do 'finger walking' - for instance, if a table tree or mountain appeared on the screen, you could walk your fingers along it, up it or across it Another trick was, if a full facial appeared on the screen, by putting your hand up and waggling your finger, you make it seem that the person was picking their nose! But I think the best was - and we all nearly got thrown out and the projectionist threatened to shut down the film - was a cowboy film, most likely John Wayne.[16] He was, naturally, chasing the 'baddies' and had his trackers with him - native Americans (or Indians as we used to call 'em). They were looking out across the desert, trying to pinpoint the baddies, and John asked on a few occasions, 'What are they doing now?' Now, this is where timing comes in. As he was saying it once again, someone put both hands up so it looked as if he was covering his eyes and at that point, he said once again, 'What are they doing now?' Some bright wag yelled out, 'Picking mushrooms.' The place erupted, Edna (Torchie) couldn't control it and that's when the projectionist (probably Mr Lewison) came flying out and threatened us all.

I believe it cost you threepence extra to sit upstairs which meant climbing all of four or five steps. As for the 'bus seats', it's claimed that half the population of Usk was conceived in/on them and as Cefn Ila – the local maternity hospital - was just up the road, they seemed to be linked! Albeit nine months later!

Fast forward a few years and the last film I saw there was a Beatles film *A Hard Day's Night*. I was not a particular fan of The Beatles. The Rolling Stones were my favourite or any of the old blues singers - Muddy Waters,[17] Howlin' Wolf,[18] Big Bill Broonzy[19] - but my real favourites were Sonny Terry[20] and Brownie McGhee.[21]

In the old days when Skiffle was King! (late 50s/early 60s), some of the local Usk lads formed a skiffle group – I don't think the group had a name. Their first gig was at the Red Shed in the afternoon prior to the film. I think there were five members but I can only remember three - Billy Hardwick, Billy Harris (my cousin), and Dickie Abbot. Dickie played the 'double bass' ie a square wooden tea chest with a broom handle and string/wire for plucking.

I remember, on one occasion, we went over to Bettws Newydd Village Hall to see a touring theatre group perform *Murder in the Red Barn*, though for the life of me, I can't remember the storyline! *Murder in the Red Barn* – obviously about someone getting murdered in a Red Barn![22]

There was a youth club held upstairs at the British Legion (this had also been the gym when we were at junior school), and another youth club at Gwehelog Parish Hall where the usual activities took place. We would pop along to the Hall Inn in Gwehelog where Jim, the landlord, would serve us with a small bottle of Babycham for which we paid 1/3pence. We then discovered that The White Hart would sell you a pint of draught cooking sherry for 5/- but you had to provide your own bottle.

Other than that, there wasn't much else to do until we were old enough to visit the pubs. The Castle pub was my local for a while. I can't remember the managers/owners who were there when I first started drinking but they had a bar skittles table and the usual dart board. Later, an ex-jockey owned it by the name of Taffy Rees who kept a few horses at ground near Lord Raglan's. Numerous pubs in Usk had shove halfpenny games, together with darts and card teams as well as bar skittles. Pubs were plentiful in Usk - about 15 in all, I believe (including clubs).[23] Like many before, we did try to visit them all in one night having a pint in each. Needless to say, we failed miserably on numerous occasions.

At one point, the Three Salmons was the only pub in Usk which would serve us. The then owner thought we were wonderful. I think he was from Porthcawl so that explains his good taste, but being rebels, we thanked him by covering the ceiling in the corner window with bumblees. Bumblees were small goblets which we fashioned out of the silver paper from cigarette packets (yep, we were allowed to smoke in pubs then). After wrapping the silver paper around a finger in the shape of goblets, we filled the base with chewed up paper, almost like rice paper. We then threw them up so that they stuck to the ceiling. At one point, that corner of the ceiling was covered in them. Whilst this was amusing to start with, we were asked to stop doing it because, when the goblets dried out sufficiently, they had the habit of falling either on to people's heads, or into their beer or food.

There was the occasional dance at the Memorial Hall or maybe a barn dance we could scrounge a lift to. If desperate we could visit the Adam and Eve club at the Bridge Inn Llangwm. This was mostly for older persons - some were as old as 40, would you believe! They had a guy who played the drums - biscuit tins - and a gramophone but hey, it was fun!

In good weather, we would make our way over to The Island next to the River Usk, with guitars, harmonicas and did the odd poem or two. We settled down near the railway bridge which was near to Splinter's Wood Yard so we had a ready supply of logs for a bonfire (sorry, Terry). We used to strum a bit and basically put the world to rights. Dylan (Bob, that is) was our inspiration then. A few of the pubs had juke boxes but we often travelled to the Tan House in Shirenewton because they had a brilliant selection of records.

If the weather was a bit inclement, we had plenty of places to spend the evening after a session in the pub. There were a couple of barns, one in the field next to the Glen yr Afon House Hotel, one on the Monmouth road near the school (the bypass cut right through the field it was in), the old Priory behind the church, and the railway station. Although the line was closed, many of the buildings remained for a few years – offices, waiting rooms, station master's office. We were able to sleep off our excesses without fear of disturbance, though we did occasionally have a visit from a local bobby on night shift who used to join us at the station rooms. We'd spend a few hours chatting and dozing. He could be a bit of a nuisance if you had a young lady with you! I don't think Sgt Dorning would have been too pleased - he was in charge of the police station at the time.

On rugby international days, we travelled to Cardiff by bus and train. We went early and spent an hour or so swimming in the Empire Pool,[24] before making our way to Cardiff Arms Park for the match. We usually bought our tickets there for the schoolboy enclosure. We had to pay a bit over the odds but hey, we were at the match!

We had a local taxi/mini-bus hire firm - Bert Thomas and his son, Clive. We would hire them to take us to Sophia Gardens in Cardiff to see bands of the day such as The Animals, Swinging Blue Jeans, plus others.

But then the Sixties kicked in big time And of course, it was the start of the hippie era so we all had beards, long hair and dressed a bit weird (that's just the fellas!).

We used to spend a fair bit of time in Bristol - much more going on there, such as busking outside the Corn Exchange and Colston Hall,[25] where the management would invite buskers in who would fill the spot whilst the band had a break. This worked well until Adge Cutler and the Wurzels came along and took over the spot![26] A group of buskers put together their own band. Basically, anyone who could play or sing could join in. They called themselves the Alligator Jug Thumpers and were great fun. In fact, they are still going today but I doubt very much if any of the original line-up are still there.

We had our own little gang, mostly three of us but we also had three others who were part-timers. We all had girlfriends I'm afraid my girlfriend's parents didn't like the people their daughter associated with – ie, me! Her father was a Borstal Officer and they banned us from seeing each other. However, this didn't stop us until her father caught us. She was afraid to go home so we ran away to Bristol where, because of previous visits by 'our gang', we knew a suitable 'Derri' (derelict shop/house) where we could hide. We stayed away for some time but eventually my two mates came and persuaded us to come home - reluctantly I might add - but I suppose it was for the best!

Because of Dylan, protesting was another interest. *Masters of War* was on everyone's lips! There was also *Don't Believe We're on the Eve of Destruction b*y Barry McGuire. There were Ban the Bomb and the Aldermaston Marches, plus the odd visit to Speakers Corner, Hyde Park. We did go on an anti-Vietnam War march from (here's where my memory shows my age !) Hereford or Ross to Monmouth and were interviewed by a reporter from *The Times,* no less!

Problem with the march was that it poured down with rain for most of the way. By the time we reached Monmouth, we were all absolutely drenched! Even our clothes had shrunk on us. Huh! Even cafés and pubs wouldn't let us in. One wimp from the Pontypool gang scrounged a lift off a passing Mini Moke so he was ostracised - our gang didn't mess about!

Aaaaah, such simple fun and times.

Chapter 11 Discipline

The usual stuff – 'Wait 'til your father gets home' from my mother – while the neighbours said, 'We know your mother and father,' (if we were caught doing something naughty).

And then there was the 'swishy stick'. This was placed in the corner by the fire. I had to get the swishy stick myself. If my mother thought it wasn't swishy enough, I had to get another one which suited her criteria!

It was waved about a bit and if deemed suitable, was placed in the corner. Only once was it used and then I was hidden in a tent (wigwam - bear in mind we were full of stories about cowboys and Indians). I'd done something wrong and went in there to hide. The tent was made out of a large old blanket and wrapped around three tent poles. I hid as far back in the tent as I could but of course my mother could see my shape (my backside jutting out) so I was given a few short sharp swipes (which, in fact, didn't hurt because of the thickness of the blanket!). Nevertheless, I made a full three-act drama out of it! Usually, if I was playing up, all she had to do was look at me, then look at the swishy stick. That was enough, I soon behaved! Not that I was ever naughty!

Chapter 12 School

Usk Council School Monmouth Road 1955.
Standards 1 and 2
L to R: Girls first: Marilyn Fear, Janice Aubrey?
Maxine Rudderham, Sally?, Frances Jones? Katherine
Price, Jennifer Jones? Dorothy Jenkins?, Monica Poynter?
Next row up: Martin Kear, Chris Rudderham, John
Jones, John Murray, Author, Graham Howells, Keith
Willis, Possibly Arwyn Knowles, Possibly Will Shapland
Top row: Mr Williams headmaster. Llewellyn Roper,
Hadrian Williams, Ronald Doxey, Michael Williams,
Johnny Smales, Miss Owers, teacher
Obviously the Rudderhams (brother and sister) were
known as Rubberbums.

I went to school in Usk – Usk Primary, the Council School. We caught a service bus from Cold Harbour, just over a mile away.

My first few days, my mother took me down to the crossroads, just along from Nyth House drive (our next-door neighbours). There, I joined forces with my cousin and other children who chaperoned us new ones to the bus stop. In those days, there wasn't a bus shelter at Cold Harbour so we had to wait for the bus in all winds and weathers. People (mostly women) say they can still remember the smell of 'steaming wet boy as they stood against the radiators to dry off'.

This bus dropped us off outside the school on the Monmouth road but for the return journey, we had to walk to the Square to catch the bus home. There, at least we could shelter in The Nag's Head porch. From the school to the Square, we had to pass the WarAg depot. Next to the school was a brick air raid shelter on which we could climb and generally make a nuisance of ourselves.[1] On the way home, I was allowed to make my own way home from the cross roads.

In 1953, for the Coronation, a few of us were privileged to be chosen to plant some trees in a grassy area just off the school yard. These trees are still there today. We also had to dress up for a 'pageant'. I remember the article with photo in *The Free Press (Pontypool),* entitled 'Usk Fairies'! (You could say you were either a Usk Butterfly or Usk Fairy!)[2]

Not long after I moved back to Usk, a few years ago, there was a school photo doing the rounds from roughly the same period. It was interesting and frustrating trying to remember the names of our classmates.

I enjoyed school and never remember the urge to 'bunk off', which was just as well because the school had a 'whipper in', a Mr Tommy Lawton, a dapper little man who always wore spats but was a real force to be reckoned with.[3] You didn't mess with Mr Lawton! To do so was at your own peril!

We were given Horlicks tablets and had a savings book on which we could save sixpence per week (2.5pence in today's money).[4] It felt great when we had saved half a crown - 2/6p!

Big school was Usk Secondary Modern *(overleaf)* in Maryport Street (formerly a Grammar School supported and financed by the Roger Edwards Trust)[5]. They had a system whereby, if you did well in your first year, you were transferred to the Grammar school proper, in Pontypool – West Mon. I enjoyed most lessons (except maths) but most of all, I enjoyed sports and especially sports day and was quite good at most sports - football, rugby, cricket, the gym.

Work at home also kept me fit! I made some lifelong pals there and still keep in touch. Other schools in Usk at the time included The Church School (boys and girls), also in Maryport Street, and a private school, Davington House, on the old Usk Chepstow road, a few hundred yards from The Olway Inn.

Chapter 13 Haymaking

Haymaking was a pretty arduous task because we had no mechanical equipment ourselves, apart from a very old tractor (Fordson Major) and a dilapidated trailer. We relied on local farmers to mow the fields for us, usually Mr Albert Heath from Llandenny Walks. We usually mowed about ten acres.

This was allowed to dry for a day or two, then it was 'turned' by hand with a large hay rake. Going around and around the field seemed an endless task. Sometimes I was on my own, other times it was my father and myself, but if we were lucky, my Uncle Aubrey and my brother-in-law Henry Rogers (Harry) would give a hand. All in all, it would take a couple of days, then a few days more to dry before we could collect it up.

It was collected by a large 'rake' pulled by the tractor and guided by Harry. The Haysweep, sometimes called a Buckrake, was pulled along the rows of hay guided by a 'driver' (our driver of the haysweep was Harry - I drove the tractor). This could be a job for a day in a 2 to 3 acre field. The wooden hay sweep was an American invention brought to England in the 1880s. Like many implements, it had its good and bad points.

The Tumbling Tam or Tumbling Tommy haysweep was used with a single steady, fast walking horse hitched with chains, using the revolving lugs at each end of the long beam. The hay was swept up from the field, running in stretches back to where the haycart stood. As the haysweep travelled, it scooped up the hay in a mounting pile. When it was full, the driver brought it to the cart and threw the handles upward, letting the horse go on walking. The sweep somersaulted forward and 'leapt' over its dropped load of hay, righted itself and was ready to collect the next load. The driver caught up the handles, walked over or round the pile of hay, and went on for another lot. Meanwhile, the men with the cart were forking the hay from the dropped load onto the cart.

We used a tractor to pull the Haysweep along but the method of loading and unloading the Haysweep is the same but to make the loading of hay quicker onto the trailer (sometimes on the same day or in the next day or so), two or three would 'pike' the hay into larger piles. Once dumped off the Rake, these haycocks were later 'piked' onto the cart. Uncle Aubrey (Harris) spread the hay on the cart to a certain level before it was transported to the rick yard.

In good weather and on flat land however, the new hay could be cleared straight from its rows. In a time of uncertain weather, ('unsettled and changeable', as the forecasters like to say), you swept the hay and collected it to make cocks - little hay stacks that could stand a bit of weather until the whole crop could be taken home. This method was in frequent use in the hillier areas with small fields and more likelihood of rain. Claude Cornfield (milkman/farmer) had a 'round baler', producing round bales rather than 'square bales'.

Gathering of hay was usually done on the weekend when more people, mostly family , were available to give a hand. There could be up to ten of us. These family members came from Usk, Newport and more local. Around about tea time, the wives and Mother brought us sandwiches and cakes, plus tea. We also had cider to drink which my father and I had collected a few days before from Harry Williams, Hollow Farm, about a mile away in Gwehelog. This was real farmhouse cider and could be rather rough!

Uncle Aubrey then built the rick because he was the best at it. There was a great skill and art in rick-making. Unless you got it right, it could topple over.

As a bottom layer, any old rough grass or bracken was used to soak up any moisture in the ground. Once the rick was deemed dry enough, galvanised sheets were used to cover it, ropes and pegs were used to secure them. If the hay wasn't as dry as it should be, there was a chance it may overheat and catch fire. My father used to test this by putting his hand as far as he could into the rick. If he gauged it was overheating, a few tin sheets were loosed, and in some case removed, allowing it to cool down.

In winter we had to cut hay from the rick for cattle feed. This involved removing one or two of the tin sheets covering the rick, climbing a ladder and cutting downwards with the hay knife. The blade of the knife was about 15 to 18 inches long. very wide and curved and extremely sharp! This task thankfully was for grown-ups only. I used to hold the 'storm lantern' during the dark nights so that my father could cut the hay. This was then carried a short distance to the hay rack in the shed, then the rick had to be re-covered - not the easiest or most pleasant of tasks during the winter months, especially during gales, rain and snow! However, the stock needed feeding and that was that! When sold, they provided a much-needed extra source of income, and to get home to a roaring coal and log open fire made it all worthwhile.

I don't remember us having to buy hay so obviously we had enough to last us through the winter.

Chapter 14 Neighbours

The Griffith family consisted of Old Bill, Annie, Young Bill and Darkie and Alf Richards, farm labourer, who was also our neighbour about 100 yards down the lane from Rose Cottage. Old Bill was known as The Fuhrer because of his 'tash. Annie used to take garden and farm produce to Pontypool Market on a Saturday, via the bus from Cold Harbour to Usk, then on to Pontypool via the Chepstow to Pontypool bus. Quite a journey to carry wicker baskets full of produce! Don't know why the gentleman was called Darkie, but he was connected to the family. They owned various properties eg Lower House and Nyth House (and the old Still House mentioned earlier), plus the land that goes with these properties.

The Jones family lived in Trostrey. Nana Jones lived at Upper House *(see opposite)*. I was always fascinated by her thatched cottage because there seemed to be birds nesting everywhere in the thatched roof, house sparrows mostly.

Nana Jones's son and three grandchildren lived at Lower House, which I often visited as the children, Alan, John and Irene, were my age and Lower House was only a couple of fields away. We were great pals. I think they had to do odd jobs for Nana Jones. I remember them using the pump to get water. There was also a well halfway down the drive which was also used. Their cousin, Jean Lewis, sometimes joined us from Usk. When she left school, she started work at Sweets Fishing Tackle Shop, then owned by an internationally known fisherman called Lionel Sweet.[1] When he died, he left the shop to Jean.[2] I still see her occasionally when I'm in Usk. I believe Alan lives in Priory Gardens and has an allotment in the Sessions House grounds.

My Uncle Ern (of Overbrook Cottage) decided to go into chicken farming and Father built three chicken houses for him. My father was a damn good carpenter. Me? I can't hit a blo*dy nail in straight. These sheds with nest boxes, above

Drawings of Upper House by Fred Hando (1888-1970)
Top: Exterior baking oven, well and pump

which were glass windows, were light and airy. They could hold a hundred chickens or more. They were built in sections, all made by my father. When Uncle Ern decided to pack this in, the sheds were lying idle for many years, until my father decided it would be good to have one of these for a garden shed! They chose the one at a place called Sunnybank along the narrow track leading to Rosebank Cottage, (Carrie Bevan's old cottage), more or less opposite Overbrook Cottage, just as you turn up the lane running alongside.

They brought the shed to our cottage. I don't know who was involved altogether. I'd been sent on holiday to a cousin's in Port Talbot to give my parents a rest! It meant dismantling the shed, approximately 30ft square, and pulling it up the bank onto the land belonging to Russel Hill Farm. From there, it was carried (by trailer) through the farmyard and onto the lane leading to Hill Farm and from there, down the road and along the top lane to Rose Cottage. This job of work was no mean feat and I believe David Morgan, Trostrey Court, did the driving and transporting of the shed to its final resting place. Once again, I don't remember the erection of this shed (holidaying again, no doubt!) but it dominated the top half of the garden. Until a few years ago, the shed was still in place at Rose Cottage and I believe one shed is still in place at Overbrook.

Chapter 15 Folklore and Medicines!

Because we were so far out of Usk, ailments were 'cured' by various ointments. For example, a cream called Fresh Liquor (often spelt 'likker'), made from calf fat, was good for chest complaints. You rubbed it on and it was supposed to ease chest pains and breathing difficulties.

The family had great faith in bread sops, chunks of bread soaked in hot milk. These bread poultices were used to 'draw' poisons and infections out, such as boils and festering splinters and thorns (usually blackthorn [Sloe], which was notorious for turning bad).

Another medicine was Black Ointment.[1] This was a cure-all. You name it, this could cure it, or so we were told! Calamine lotion was also used a lot, especially for measles.

Bicarb (bicarbonate of soda) was used to clear up indigestion. Bicarb actually works much better than any of the propriety brands for indigestion relief. A pinch of bicarb was also added to green vegetables to maintain their 'greenness', otherwise boiling drained the colour. Mustard and/or pepper were rubbed on gums and teeth to ease toothache, and salt was used to clean teeth.

Blue bags (small sachets), used for whitening shirts etc, were also used to treat wasp stings.[2]

My mother suffered badly from asthma for which she needed 'her pump'. This was a rubber ball connected to a spray to which you could attach a small glass bottle about 3inches in length (dark green and ribbed with a label stating 'Poison'). This was attached to another tube, then, by squeezing the rubber ball, a spray was directed into your mouth, thus relieving her breathing difficulties. Mother usually suffered worse at Christmas time, because of her feathering activities with the chickens.

Of course, the chemist provided all the usual medicines and pills such as aspirin, cough medicine and Vick (used a lot for bad chests). You could also buy cyanide from the chemist which was used to kill wasps (nests).

I did suffer the usual childhood illnesses but rarely were we bedbound. There was too much to do, work and playwise.

Although not a herbalist, I am very interested in plants, either their medicinal uses, folklore or their habitat requirements. The old ones used to refer to the book *The Doctrine of Signatures* which basically suggested that if any part of a plant resembled a body part – internally or externally – it could help cure or offer relief from pain if applied in a variety of forms. I tend to refer to Nicholas Culpeper's (1616-1654) *Complete Herbal* because I quite like his philosophy. If you didn't have the wherewithal to cover the cost of his advice, he was quite prepared to take payment in kind - fruit, eggs, meat, vegetables - for which he was ridiculed by many of his peer group. In the Civil War, he fought on the Parliamentary side. Well, I suppose no one's perfect!

Growing up in the country we were told what plants were beneficial and more importantly the ones we should leave alone! Dandelions for example would make you 'wet the bed' (it is actually a diuretic) and leaves a nasty stain on your hands/fingers, as would the green soft outer casing of walnuts. You could eat the newly emerging leaves of the hawthorn known as 'bread and cheese'. Elderflower wine was seen as a bit of cure all (?) and hot, it was good to make you 'sweat out' colds and flu. It was also good as an eyewash.

Garlic mustard is a member of the cabbage family but is the only one to give off a garlicky-type smell, also known as Jack by the hedge. Used mainly as a condiment, it can be used medicinally for relief of colic and asthma, it's also a diuretic. Its seeds are one the food plants of the orange tip butterfly caterpillar.

Ground ivy was used in brewing to 'sharpen' the taste of the ale. Hence it was known to the 'old ones' as Alehoof. The leaves are slightly mint scented and can be infused in boiling water and is reputed to relieve coughs and chest disorders and was often sold by street vendors, in London especially.

Any plant which has 'wort' or 'officinalis' in its name means that it is useful medicinally. For example, stitchwort (greater stitchwort) - the stems break easily, therefore it must be good for mending broken bones and can also be used to cure 'the stitch', provided it's mixed with acorns and wine! Comfrey was also known by the 'old ones' as 'knitbone' because, once again , it had the ability to mend bones.

Meadow sweet is very fragrant. Known originally as mede-sweet, it was used to help flavour mead. It was also known as 'courtship and marriage' because of the sweet scent of its flowers representing courting, whilst the sharp smell of its crushed leaves depicted the realism of marriage. If you had nobility visiting, the sweet-smelling flowers were strewn over the floor in an attempt to mask the odour of medieval smells.

There are many other plants with myths, legends and folklore attached, with fascinating explanations as to how they came by their name(s). Enchanters' nightshade can protect you against evil spirits. Its Latin name *Circaea* refers to the sorceress Circe who tempted one of the Greek Gods to abandon his round the world trip! Figwort was used as a dye and the gipsies call it the 'queen of the herbs'. The small flowers are much sought after by Queen wasps. Ground elder or whiteash was also known as 'goutweed' because the species name translated from the Greek means 'gout' It was at one time used as a spinach-type vegetable and when eaten with butter, was considered a delicacy. Herb Robert has red flowers and in certain conditions, its leaves and stems will turn red. Thus it was seen as a cure for blood disorders. Blackberries should not be eaten after Michaelmas - September 29 - because the Devil has spat on them. There are over 2,000 microspecies so that's one h*lluva lot of spit!

The lowly celandine is known as pilewort because some the roots are covered with nodules. However, the plant called Greater celandine *(Chelidonium majus)* - no relation at all to the common celandine - produces orange sap which was good for getting rid of warts (it does work).

The old favourite, dock leaves, were essential for nettle stings.

The Romans are blamed for introducing many 'alien' species to Britain but anything they considered worthless, they prefixed with 'dog' eg dog rose, dog violet, dogwood, dog mercury. Most plants have many local names but to make sure naturalists, and botanists especially, knew what others were talking about, the Swedish naturalist Linnaeus provided the genus and the species, which is why plants have two scientific names. To ensure there is no confusion when local names are used, for identification proper, you quoted the full scientific name.

The cuckoo pint or wild arum has numerous other local names. It takes on a sexual connotation! 'Pint' is a corruption of the old English word 'pintle' which refers to a certain part of male genitalia. The spathe (hood) is somehow connected to a husband being cuckolded (the pintle hiding in the hood clandestinely). Corms or tubers were used as whitening when washing clothes, especially aprons, but it did have a very bad effect on your hands.

Looking through the herbal books of which there are quite a few, it would seem that, in centuries past, women suffered a great deal of melancholy whereas men seemed to need the use of aphrodisiacs. Was there a connection here, I wonder?

Local folklore always insisted you should never sit with your back to the fire because it would make you sick! I used to have a seat in the corner of the hearth, just at the end of the fender, and was always told off because I was sure to get chilblains (I never did).

We were warned not to kill spiders. If we did, we would make it rain. Here's another spider one:
If you want to prosper and thrive,
Let a spider run alive.
Another rhyme my Mother taught me was,

A little Robin and a Wren
Are God Almighty's cock and hen'.

Woe betide us if we hurt, killed either of these two!
I often wonder where the 'old ones' gleaned their knowledge from, handed down from generation to generation, I suppose, though that doesn't explain where it all started. One saying that was often used when a married couple were starting a family was 'a pigeon pair' if they only wanted two children. Apparently, pigeons only lay two eggs which hatch into one male and one female, hence pigeon pair! Where my parents learned this from, I've no idea, because, although they knew the names of many birds, they were not by any stretch of the imagination 'birders' and pigeons are not the easiest to identify male from female! But someone somewhere must have done a study on them which became common knowledge.

Chapter 16 Trostrey Characters and Eccentrics

Trostrey, like every other community, had its share of scandals and neighbourly disputes as well as its community spirit. There were also a few characters and eccentrics, for example, Old Arthur , Celia (Cecelia(?) and Miss Llewellyn, to name but a few!

Old Arthur lived in an old cottage on the side of the road to Russel Hill and Hill Farm. It was pretty much tumbled down and apparently there was only one room in which Arthur lived and slept because of the leaking roof.

Arthur could be described as a tramp with living accommodation. He used to wander the lanes any time of the day and night with his sack on his back. What it contained no-one knew but it must have meant a lot to him. Nobody is sure where he came from, other than 'from the valleys'. It is believed he came from a wealthy family who provided pit props for the mines. How he came to live at Trostrey, again no-one seemed to know.

He had an annoying habit of always walking in the shadows at night or sitting on the bank or verges under a suitable tree, especially at the bottom of the lane leading up to Rose Cottage. As you passed by (without noticing him), he would greet you with *'G'Night, Boy'*, having had one or two pints at the Hall Inn in Gwehelog. This used to frighten the life out of me but you got used to it and would automatically say *'G' Night, Arthur'* as you passed. He would either answer or not, obviously depending on if he was there. However, on occasions, he would change his resting place. If I had no response from his usual place, I would wander on up the lane, when suddenly you would hear *'G'Night, Boy'*. I used to berate him, saying words to the effect, *'Blinking 'eck, Arthur, you frightened the life out of me'*. This he found highly amusing! I could still hear him laughing as I got further up the lane. Arthur was placed in a 'Home' near

Nant-y-deri. A few locals from Trostrey and Gwehelog visited him occasionally and he seemed to like it there.

He did occasional work, gardening etc, for the Llewellyns who lived at Glyn Heulog(?) at Llancayo, Daphne Llewellyn used to drive an old soft top Alvis car She once ran over Arthur's foot and then berated him for having his foot in the way! On another occasion, she parked in the main street of Usk outside Bowyers, just as a policeman was walking by.[1] She told him in no uncertain terms not to 'book her', which he didn't, either through fear or servitude! Whenever her name was mentioned, it was always followed by 'she lived in London for a long time'. What this signified I never really found out but it was followed by a 'knowing' look and a nudge wink. She was an accomplished artist and you would often see her sitting in the middle of a field with her paints and easel, painting the scenery.

There was a local farmer who had a small farm near Gwehelog Village Hall. Cruelly, (but then, children are, aren't they?) his nickname was Drady Williams. Because of a speech impediment, he put 'dr' in front of most words when he was speaking.

He was having a moan about the amount of traffic on the roads (this is about 60 years ago - I know, I know, I was a babe in arms! I wish !!) I remember him speaking to my father about a near miss he had had with a car coming along the lane. 'An I drood in the droad like a drummy,' he told us. (Translates as – 'And I stood in the road like a dummy'.) I've no idea what happened to him – whether he died or moved - but he was well known for this impediment

Celia/Cecelia lived at Walnut Tree and was a little old lady who always dressed in black or purple and wore hobnail boots. I'm sure the poem *When I am old I will wear purple'* was written for her![2] At first, she lived with her mother and often used to push her around the garden in a wheelbarrow! Another passion of hers was to rush outside whenever a plane flew over, waving her walking stick and shouting obscenities at it. She always seemed to be surrounded by cats. As children, we used to look through the gate, basically to wind her up. She would come clattering up the driveway, yelling and waving her stick at us which we thought was great fun! I don't know what happened to Celia or her mother.

A lady lived in one of the cottages at the bottom of Cold Harbour. I'm not sure how to put this delicately, but she used to entertain lorry drivers – bear in mind this was the main road for traffic until the dual carriageway was built. They used to pick her up somewhere near her cottage, drive to a lay-by(!) and have a 'chat'! He would then take her a bit further along, she would cross the road and hitch a lift with a lorry back to her cottage, having had another 'chat' on the way home.

Please bear in mind the following events happened over 60 years ago!

Two of our neighbours conducted an illicit affair which was well known throughout the community and was viewed with a certain amount of hilarity and a good source of gossip amongst young and old alike.

For the purposes of this tale, I will call them Samson and Edina. They lived approximately a mile apart. Samson lived in a caravan with his wife and Edina lived in a cottage with her husband, not far from Rose Cottage.

They met usually once a week at a given time. The place for this clandestine meeting was a rather large unused chicken coop in a field about halfway between their properties. As children, we got to know what days and time they met, albeit purely by chance. We had better things to do, like climbing trees, fishing in the brook and wandering around in the woods, than listen to smutty gossip and the goings on of the above couple, as shared by neighbours and family, which we didn't fully understand at any rate!

However, having watched both of them arriving for one of their 'meetings', we decided – myself and a few friends –

that it would be good fun to surprise them, so, on a certain day at a given time, we hid behind a hedge and some bushes, just a matter of a stone's throw – literally! - from the Chicken Cot. Edina arrived first, shortly followed by Samson. We gave them about five minutes, then started throwing stones (we had come prepared!) which went clattering onto the sheeted roof. We followed this up with whoops, yells and whistles – one of our 'gang' had just learned to whistle by putting fingers in his mouth so this added to the bedlam! Samson came charging out of the door yelling obscenities at us. Unfortunately, because his trousers were somewhat in disarray, he didn't get very far but he kept his modesty by still wearing his Long Johns. (Please bear in mind this was a time before Y Fronts and Boxer Shorts. You had two pairs of long johns, one for summer and one for winter. In those days, men also wore sock suspenders to keep their socks up. These fitted just above the calf muscle with straps hanging down to attach to the socks. They were only worn on special occasions!). We ran away yelling and making rude signs until Samson gave up the chase, which wasn't very far, and we left them in peace then to carry on with their meeting.

News of our escapade leaked out and we were a hit with school friends, and eventually our families, and we were asked to repeat the tale of this escapade to other members of our family and friends which gave a certain amount of kudos and notoriety to 'our gang'.

After a few years, Samson and his wife moved to Newport so everyone thought that that would be the end of the affair between him and Edina. Wrong! Love will always find a way and suddenly Edina decided that going to the 'pictures' on a Saturday night in Newport was a way to brighten up her life.

On her way home, usually about 10.30pm, (Yes! Buses did run at night in those days! I remember the last bus from Newport to Monmouth left at about 10pm.) We knew roughly what time she was near our cottage because the dog would bark and we would put the outside light on for her to see down the lane. She would then pop in for a cuppa.

At the time, we had one of the old upright pianos and, without any encouragement, Edina would play popular songs of the day and much older ones. These 'soirees' soon became known amongst our neighbours and on a Saturday night, half a dozen or so would turn up for a singalong (and the occasional poem) which usually lasted until midnight. Songs such as *My Grandfather's Clock, Little Brown Jug, The Old Rugged Cross* were firm favourites, along with *When Father Painted the Parlour, To be a Farmers Boy, The Fox is away to his Den-o, Goodnight Irene, Bluebells We'll Gather.* One I can remember was about Mary Ellen:

> *Mary Ellen at the church turned up*
> *Her Ma turned up*
> *An' her Pa turned up.*
> *Her sister Gert*
> *An' her rich uncle Bert*
> *And the parson in his long white shirt turned*
> *up.*
> *But no bridegroom with the ring turned up*
> *But a telegram boy with his nose turned up*
> *Brought a telegram that read*
> *That he didn't want to wed*
> *And they found him in the river*
> *With his toes turned up.*[3]

(They don't write 'em like that anymore!)

Others included *Down by the Ash Grove, Song of Little Mary* (a very sad song which used to make me cry), *Nellie Dean, Will the Angels Way up Yonder Play Their Harps for Me, Apple Blossom Time, In Dublin's Fair City, If I were a Blackbird, I'd whistle and sing.* For this, one of the 'audience' would start to whistle like a blackbird – supposedly!

Poems such as:

> *Poor little piggywig, Poor little swine*
> *Sage and onion up his b*m ...*

As children we loved this one because of the naughty word. Another one about flatulence is far too crude to print but we insisted that one of the men recite it, once again because of the naughty words.

About halfway through these proceedings, Mother would bring out the tea and sandwiches - bread and cheese with beetroot and onion dip. Depending on whether we had recently killed a pig, there would be ham, boiled bacon or brawn, all accompanied by salad and/or boiled new potatoes.

To end this tale, Edina and her husband moved to Usk so we saw very little of them. What happened to Samson and his wife we never knew.

Chapter 17 Work

I eventually started work at BNS (British Nylon Spinners), which eventually became ICI Fibres, based at Mamhilad. After a few years, I left home and my job and went walkabout - well, it was the Sixties.

As hippies, we decided to start our walkabout in Jersey, flower picking, strawberry picking and spud picking, and cleaning cars. When strawberry picking, the owner told us to eat as many as wanted. We needed no second bidding! After a few days of gorging, we were sickened by the sight of strawberries but of course it was the holiday season so what did everyone have after a meal? Bl*ody strawberries! Then London called, so off we went.

Life eventually took over. I got married, produced two children, both boys. Unfortunately, the marriage floundered and we divorced so I brought up the two boys on my own. However, later on, my ex-wife was a supporter of the Greenham Common Women's protest movement. Men could become honorary women and help with household chores such as cooking but you could only enter the site through Gate Orange.

The last march or protest I went on was the Newbury By-pass demo about 25 years ago. I travelled down with members of Gwent Ornithological Society. We had the pleasure of being introduced to 'Swampy', a young activist who's still protesting!

When I first started the Usk Conservation and Environmental Group, a lad who used to join us on our guided walks programme had a job at Newport Wetlands. However, for some reason, he decided to move and moved to somewhere near Greenham Common He became a warden there because the site had now become a Nature Reserve. He invited UCEG members to visit for a guided tour which would have been nice, just to see how it had developed over the years but I'm afraid it was a case of the old adage 'best laid plans of mice and men....' So it never materialised.

I also palled up with a local gentleman with rather left-wing Socialist views - Ike Evans, local farmer - who farmed along Factory Lane. Ike and I spent many an hour sorting out the world's problems. He was a very erudite gentleman and I learnt a h*lluva lot from him and not just on a political front.

But I kept my love of singalongs and poetry, all stemming from those nights of so many, many years ago. For my sins, I now run a Folk, Blues and Country Music club in Abergavenny - Purely Acoustic - which also includes poetry - our own efforts or by other well-known poets - and I always insist that the last quarter of an hour or so, we have a singalong of up-to-date anthemic/chorus-driven songs, such as *Hotel California, Lying Eyes, Wild Mountain Thyme, Mighty Quinn* etc. I insist on audience participation. Everyone must join in, players and audience, which does seem to go down well.

In ancient times, about a century and a half ago (!), it was customary for factory owners and bosses to provide their workers with a glass of ale in the workplace, basically, to keep them sweet and take their minds off bad working conditions, low pay and long hours. However, there was always going to be an unscrupulous boss who would take advantage of such a generous act! Below is traditional song which was penned to enlighten the workers and public in general about such unscrupulous behaviour.

The Man that Waters the Workers' Beer[1]

Chorus
Now I'm the man, the very fat man , that
waters the workers' beer
Yes, I'm the man, the very fat man, that waters
the workers' beer
And what do I care if it makes them ill, or
makes them terribly queer

I've a car , a yacht and an aeroplane and I waters the workers' beer

Now when I makes the workers' beer , I puts in strychnine
Some methylated spirits and a drop of paraffin
But since a brew so terribly strong might make them terribly queer
I reaches my hand for the water tap, And I waters the workers' beer

(Chorus)

Now ladies fair and beyond compare, and be ye maid or wife,
O, sometimes lend a thought for one who leads a sorry life;
The water rates are shockingly high, and malt is shockingly dear,
And there isn't the profit there used to be in wat'ring the workers' beer

(Chorus)

Now a drop of good beer is good for a man who's thirsty tired and hot,
And I sometimes has a drop for myself from a very special pot;
But a fat and healthy working class is the thing that I most fear,
So I reaches my hand for the water tap, And I waters the workers' beer
(Chorus)

End

Irish Ballad[2]

About a maid I'll sing a song
Rickety- tickety – tin
Who did not have her family long
Not only did she do them wrong
She did every one of them in, them in
She did every one of them in

One morning in a fit of pique
Rickety –tickety- tin
She threw her father in the creek
The water tasted bad for a week
We had to make do with gin, with gin
We had to make do with gin

Her mother she could never stand
Rickety –tickety- tin
And so a cyanide soup was planned
Her mother died with a spoon in hand
And her face in a hideous grin, a grin
Her face in and hideous grin

She set her sister's hair on fire
Rickety –tickety- tin
And as the flames grew higher and higher
She danced around the funeral pyre
Playing her violin,– olin
Playing her violin

She tied her brother down with stones
Rickety –tickety- tin
And sent him off to Davy Jones
All they ever found were bones
And occasional pieces of skin, of skin
Occasional pieces of skin

One morning she had nothing to do
Rickety –tickety- tin
She sawed her baby brother in two
And put him an Irish stew
And invited the neighbours in, them in
Invited the neighbours in

About a week the police came by
Rickety –tickety- tin
Her terrible deeds she did not deny
To do so would have been a lie
And lying she knew was a sin, a sin
Lying she knew was a sin

This very sad tale I won't prolong
Rickety –tickety- tin
An if you think I went on too long
Blame yourselves for letting me go on
You should never have let me begin, begin
You should never have let me begin.

ABOUT THE AUTHOR

Graham returned to live in Usk about 25 years ago, having spent the previous 30 years going walkabout.

He lived at his childhood home, Rose Cottage, for a while before moving to Usk with his partner Jill. He decided to take up education again as a mature student and enrolled at Usk College on a course covering environment, conservation and woodland management. From there, he went to the University of South Wales, gaining a BA Hons degree in Environmental and Geography Studies. He followed that with an MA course on Upland Ecology, all managed with the love and support of Jill who continues to support him in the endeavours he currently enjoys.

He set up the Usk Conservation and Environmental Group which is still very active around Usk town today.

They moved from Usk to a 16-acre property next to the canal on the side of the Blorenge Mountain just above Llanfoist. Jill had always had an interest in horses so they decided, with the ground spare, that rescuing neglected, abused and ill-treated horses would occupy their time. Currently they have five - four mini-Shetlands and one full Shetland which is only on loan! A rescued Golden Guernsey goat by the name of Marigold shares the land with the horses.

Graham runs a folk club in Abergavenny, is a member of Black Mountain Jazz and Abergavenny Poetry Group, as well as taking part in Open Mic sessions, usually doing poetry.

About the Publishers

Saron Publishers has been in existence for about fourteen years, producing niche magazines. Our first venture into books took place in 2016 when we published *The Meanderings of Bing* by Tim Harnden-Taylor. Further publications include *Minstrel Magic,* by Eleanor Pritchard, George Mitchell's biography, *Penthusiasm,* a collection of short stories and poems from Penthusiasts, a writing group based in the beautiful town of Usk, and *Frank,* a gentle novel about loss, by Julie Hamill. Its sequel *Jackie* was published in 2019.

2021 will see the publication of Darcy Drummond's third novel, *High Manor,* following the successful *Summer Season* and *Water of Life.* Kevin Moore's third book, *Good Cop Bad Cop,* follows his successful previous books, *Real Murder Investigations – An Insider's View* and *My Way.* David Kenny's *Newport Operatic Society – the First One Hundred Years,* published in April 2021, quickly became a best seller.

Why not join our mailing list by emailing info@saronpublishers.co.uk. We promise no spam ever.

Visit our website saronpublishers.co.uk to keep up to date and to read reviews of what we've been reading and enjoying. You can also enjoy the occasional offer of a free Bing chapter.

Follow us on Facebook @saronpublishing.

Follow us on Twitter @saronpublishers.

Notes

Chapter 1 Trostrey

[1] The last people to be transported to Australia were James Solomons and Henry Williams. On 2nd January 1866, both were sentenced together at Usk Quarter Sessions to 10 years transportation, and left Britain on the *Norwood* in 1867. There seems to be no record of their crime but it was obviously a joint enterprise of some kind and so could well have been the making of illicit liquor.

[2] Rosie Humphreys, custodian of Usk Castle, reports: Henry's father Rudge (her father-in-law) bought a cauldron many years ago that was no use as it had a hole in it. Henry got the big cast iron still that is outside our house from the same place, Griffiths The Hill farm, about 30 years ago, but the distilling parts are missing. Still House was on the farm in a hidden valley near Upper Berllwyd, but was pulled down before Henry's time. I tease visitors to guess what the still is (looks like a bomb but...). The cauldron is under the mulberry tree in the Herb Garden, with a hole in it, smashed by Customs and Excise, so the story goes. The owners were rewarded with a one-way ticket to Australia, it is said.

Chapter 2 Family History

[1] The Princess Mary Gift Fund box was an embossed brass box that originally contained a variety of items such as tobacco and chocolate. It was given as a Christmas present to those serving at Christmas in 1914 and was paid for by a public fund backed by Princess Mary, the only daughter of George V and Queen Mary.

[2] Roy Saunders, in *A Monmouthshire Windmill Ruin*, says: 'Edward Berry, after years of privateering and sacking of French ships, during the Napoleonic Wars, suddenly took a turn for agriculture and settled down in the Vale of Usk, where he built the mill and nearby farms.' Sadly, this tale seems to have been caused by confusion between Edward Berry, who did indeed fight in the Napoleonic Wars with Nelson, and Edward Berry who was a prosperous velvet merchant from Yorkshire. The latter married a Huguenot lady in London and they had two daughters, Louisa and Jane. Tragically, while they were visiting their family in

France at the time of the French Revolution, Mrs Berry was captured and guillotined. Mr Berry and his daughters managed to escape. It was after this that he moved to Wales where he built up the Llancayo Estate which included Llancayo House and the Windmill.

Chapter 4 Utilities

[1] A brand name for a type of chemical toilet These toilets are usually, but not always, self-contained and movable. It is structured around a relatively small tank, which needs to be emptied frequently. It is not connected to a hole in the ground (like a pit latrine), nor to a septic tank, nor is it plumbed into a municipal system leading to a sewage treatment plant.

[2] Water was actually pumped from the Prioress Mill Pumping Station, at The Radyr, on the south bank of the River Usk. The water was abstracted from the river and pumped to Llandegfedd Reservoir, before being treated at Sluvad Water Treatment Works.

Chapter 5 Usk

[1] Erected in 1887 by public subscription in honour of Queen Victoria's Jubilee 1887. It was moved to its present position in the 1970s from its original site near the chapel. It's a free-standing square column in red brick supporting a four-sided clock.

[2] The origins of the pub date back to the 15th century when Twyn Square was the town's bustling market place. Known as the Pen Cefyl (Welsh for 'Horses Head'), it was later a coaching inn, as well as a place for local people to enjoy a jug of ale. Although the Nag's Head no longer offers overnight accommodation, its purpose has not really changed that much over the centuries. In the 1960s the pub was bought by the Key Family and has been under their ownership and management for 52 years.

[3] Now a private house.

[4] Also now a private house.

[5] The Olway Inn dates back to the 17th century and still retains its traditional pub charm with an attractive beamed bar and open fire.

⁶ Also still a pub.

⁷ This is now a Pilates studio.

⁸ A 17ᵗʰ century coaching inn which remains a hotel.

⁹ Now the White Hare Gin Distillery.

¹⁰ Now a private house.

¹¹ Now a hair salon, barbers and an ice cream parlour.

¹² Sadly this has been closed for many years.

¹³ This remains a pub and dates back to 1588.

¹⁴ Also still a pub. The main body of the property was constructed circa 1368 and it became established as a public house during the 1830s. The lounge bar has a magnificent fireplace where the original mantle can still be seen on either side within the stone walls. The exposed beams in the bar and in several of the bedrooms are original ship timbers sourced from the nearby city of Newport. The bar server itself was once a large fireplace and the arch in the centre of it is what remains of the old chimney. The hallway leading on from the bar is home to a mullion in the wall which features iron bars. Now the cellar, this used to house condemned prisoners before they were taken to the gallows to be hung. The gallows were situated on the town bridge.

¹⁵ No longer a pub.

¹⁶ This remains a pub.

¹⁷ The Sessions House is a Victorian courthouse designed by Thomas Henry Wyatt in 1877. It is a Grade Two Listed Building. It originally contained two courtrooms but Court Number 1 was gutted by fire in 1944 and was not re-built. Court Number 2 survives little altered. There is an impressive judge's chair and the benches retain their original labels for Counsel, Solicitors, Reporters, Jury etc. A passage under the dock leads through to Usk Prison which stands next door. The Sessions House saw two major nineteenth century trials: those of Margaret Mackworth, a prominent suffragette; and of Josef Garcia, a Spanish seaman, who was tried and convicted of the murder of William and Elizabeth Watkins of Llangybi and of their three youngest children Charlotte, Alice and Frederick in 1878, though serious doubt is now cast on his guilt. The building was purchased by Usk Town Council to mark the Millennium, and it is now used as the town hall and for

community use. Because of the excellent state of its preservation, it is in great demand as a film location.

18 The Memorial Hall was built as a tribute to those who lost their lives in the two world wars. It was opened in September 1960. The Memorial Hall garden in the front of the hall was developed from a piece of waste ground owned by the Hall, in the 1990s, as a quiet place to sit for anyone who has suffered loss. There is a bench remembering young Wyn Jones, who died aged 6 in a tragic farming accident, and a lamp in remembrance of George Hathaway who oversaw the rejuvenation of the hall at this time.

19 Usk Prison was built in 1841/2 and extended in 1868. It opened in 1844 as a House of Correction, and after the addition of other buildings in 1870, the establishment became the Monmouthshire County Gaol, superseding the gaol in Monmouth. It retained that role until 1922 when it closed, reopening in 1939 as a borstal. It continued in that role until 1964 when it became a Detention Centre. In 1983 Usk became a Youth Custody Centre and from 1988 to 1990 a Young Offenders Institution. In May 1990, it became an Adult Category C prison for Vulnerable Prisoners (mainly sex offenders) and it continues in that role today. The building received a Grade II* heritage listing in 1974.

Chapter 6 Food
1 The urinary bladder of a domestic pig, similar to the human urinary bladder.

Chapter 7 Clothing
1 A person who sells goods on credit, especially from door to door.

2 One of the leading providers of fairground rides, attractions and family entertainment throughout the West of England, Wales and beyond. The company is currently run by the fifth generation of Danters.

Chapter 8 Chores

[1] Rennet is an enzyme used to break the solid particles in milk away from the water content in order to form a solid mass. Mainly used to make cheese.

Chapter 9 Play and Friends

[1] A British illustrator and comics artist. She was known for her cute, nostalgic drawings of children, based on her daughter, Peggy. Her drawings are featured on many postcards, advertisements, posters, books and figurines.

[2] In 1940, faced with the prospect of a German invasion, Usk, like other local places, had a (highly secret) Auxiliary Unit. Made up of specially trained local men, their task was simple. In the event of a German invasion, they were to melt away from their civilian jobs to activate OBs (operational bases) and sabotage enemy installations for as long as possible before detection - and inevitable death. Each of the Monmouthshire Units had a biblical name. Usk's was 'Esau'. The OBs were no mere dugouts. Carefully chosen for proximity to a natural water supply and to roads, they also boasted some clever ventilation arrangements. It had an entrance from which steps ran down to a small room. A concrete pipe then ran through to a larger room with bunk beds and a corrugated iron roof. Another pipe, the escape tunnel, led out to an area of bramble bushes. Like so many members of WWII secret operations, the Auxiliaries remained silent and unrecognised for years afterwards. Even when their role was finally disclosed, they were often portrayed as little more than a leaner, meaner version of *Dad's Army*.

[3] A variable-ratio bicycle gearing system consisting of a chain, multiple sprockets of different sizes and a mechanism to move the chain from one sprocket to another. Although referred to as gears in the bike world, derailleurs are technically sprockets since they drive or are driven by a chain, and are not driven by one another.

[4] The longest running British children's comic magazine, published by DC Thomson. The comic first appeared on 30 July 1938, and was published weekly. In September 2009,*The Beano*'s 3,500th issue was published.Its weekly circulation in April 1950 was 1,974,072.

5 A British children's comic magazine published by DC Thomson. The first issue was printed in December 1937, making it the world's third-longest running comic. It reached sales of two million a week in the 1950s.

6 A British children's comic, first published from 1950 to 1969, and then in a relaunched format from 1982 to 1994.

7 The brand name for a range of die-cast zinc alloy miniature vehicles produced by Meccano. Made from 1934 to 1979, they were among the most popular diecast vehicles ever made and are highly collectible.

8 This book was first published privately in 1928 in Italy and in 1929 in France. An unexpurgated edition was not published openly in the UK until 1960, when it was the subject of a watershed obscenity trial against the publisher Penguin Books, which won the case and quickly sold three million copies. The book was also banned in the United States, Canada, Australia, India and Japan. It soon became notorious for its story of the physical (and emotional) relationship between a working class man and an upper class woman, its explicit descriptions of sex and its use of then-unprintable four-letter words.

9 Bulmers is one of the biggest selling British bottled cider brands in the UK, with a number of variants including Bulmers Original & Pear.

10 Fitzroy Richard Somerset, 4th Baron Raglan (1885-1964) was a British soldier, author, and amateur anthropologist. His books include *The Hero, A Study in Tradition, Myth and Drama* and *Monmouthshire Houses,* with Cyril Fox. Cefn Tilla Court is now run as a wedding venue.

11 A small perennial herb, whose underground part resembles a chestnut and is sometimes eaten as a wild or cultivated root vegetable.

Chapter 10 Entertainment

1 Anne Shelton OBE was a popular English vocalist, who is remembered for providing inspirational songs for soldiers both on radio broadcasts, and in person, at British military bases during the Second World War. Shelton was also the original British singer of the Lale Andersen German love-song *Lili Marlene.*

2 It is published as having been written by Bob Merrill in 1952 and loosely based on the folk tune *Carnival of Venice*. This song is also loosely based on the song *Oh, Where, Oh, Where Has My Little Dog Gone?'* The best-known version of the song was the original, recorded by Patti Page in 1952. It reached No 1 on both the *Billboard* and *Cash Box* Charts in 1953, and sold over two million copies. The recording by Lita Roza was the one most widely heard in the UK, reaching No. 1 on the UK Singles Chart in 1953. It distinguished Roza as the first British woman to have a number-one hit in the UK chart. It was also the first song with a question in the title to reach number 1.

3 A BBC Radio producer and presenter. He became known as Uncle Mac on *Children's Hour* and *Children's Favourites* and was the voice of Larry the Lamb in *Toytown*. He was the head of children's broadcasting for the BBC from 1933 until 1951.

4 An American singer, actor, and television host. Known as the King of the Cowboys, he appeared in over 100 films and numerous radio and television episodes of *The Roy Rogers Show*.

5 The British Forces Post Office (BFPO) provides a postal service to HM Forces, separate from that provided by Royal Mail.

6 A British radio and television domestic sitcom which ran from 1950–1961 on radio, 1955–1960 on television. It featured a real American family. Ben Lyon and his wife Bebe Daniels had settled in London during WWII and featured with Austrian-born British actor and comedian Vic Oliver in the radio series *Hi Gang!* that ran from 1940 to 1949.

7 A British sitcom that aired on ITV for three series from 1960 to 1963, with a fourth in 1974. The show is a spin-off of *The Army Game*, a sitcom about soldiers undertaking National Service, and follows two of the main characters (played by Alfie Bass and Bill Fraser) after they returned to civilian life.

8 Originally produced by ATV for the ITV network from 1955 to 1969, it went by its original name *Sunday Night at the London Palladium* from 25 September 1955 until the name was changed to *The London Palladium Show* from 1966 to 1969. After the Tiller Girls and the lesser acts in the first part was a game show imported from America, *Beat the Clock,* which featured couples having to perform a trick or stunt. If

a couple could complete both stunts, the wife must rearrange words into a well known phrase or saying in 30 seconds. If she succeeded, the couple won a major prize. Whenever a bell rang, the couple who played at that time would play a jackpot stunt for a cash bonus worth £100 for each week since the last jackpot win. The second part of the show featured many top people over the years including Bill Haley, Chubby Checker and Sammy David Jr. Other star guests included Judy Garland, Bob Hope, Johnnie Ray, Liberace, Petula Clark, the Seekers, the Beatles and the Rolling Stones.

9 An English comedian, actor and vocalist of popular songs. He is remembered for screen roles such as the corrupt policeman Parky in the British gangster film *The Long Good Friday* (1980) and Clifford Duckworth in *Coronation Street*.

10 An English radio and television presenter, game show host and actor.

11 A British Quiz show hosted by Hughie Green. Originally broadcast on Radio Luxembourg since 1950 and based on American radio quiz *Take It Or Leave It* in 1940–1947, it transferred to ITV in 1955, a few days after the commercial channel began broadcasting.

12 A Canadian-American singer, songwriter, and actor. Anka became famous with hit songs like *Diana, Lonely Boy, Put Your Head on My Shoulder* and *(You're) Having My Baby*. He wrote such well-known music as the theme for *The Tonight Show Starring Johnny Carson* and one of Tom Jones' biggest hits *She's a Lady*. He also wrote the English lyrics to Claude Francois and Jacques Revaux's music for Frank Sinatra's signature song *My Way*. Two songs he co-wrote with Michael Jackson, *This is It* and *Love Never Felt So Good*, became posthumous hits for Jackson.

13 A 1952 American film, produced and directed by Cecil B DeMille.

14 Fictional New York City characters, portrayed by a company of New York actors, who were the subject of feature films released from 1946 through 1958.

15 The English comic actor, filmmaker, and composer who rose to fame in the era of silent films. He became a worldwide icon through his screen persona, The Tramp, and is considered one of the most important figures in the history

of the film industry. His career spanned more than 75 years, from childhood in the Victorian era until a year before his death in 1977, and encompassed both adulation and controversy.

[16] The American actor and filmmaker who became a popular icon through his starring roles in Western films. His career spanned from the silent era of the 1920s, through the Golden Age of Hollywood and eventually American New Wave, appearing in a total of 179 film and television productions. He was among the top box office draws for three decades, and appeared with many other important Hollywood stars of his era.

[17] McKinley Morganfield (1913–1983), known professionally as Muddy Waters, was an American Blues singer-songwriter and musician who was an important figure in the post-war blues scene, and is often cited as the father of modern Chicago blues.

[18] A Chicago blues singer, guitarist, and harmonica player. Originally from Mississippi, he moved to Chicago in adulthood and became successful, forming a rivalry with fellow bluesman Muddy Waters. With a booming voice and imposing physical presence, he is one of the best-known Chicago blues artists.

[19] An American Blues singer, songwriter and guitarist. His career began in the 1920s, when he played country blues to mostly African-American audiences. Through the 1930s and 1940s he successfully navigated a transition in style to a more urban blues sound popular with working-class African-American audiences. In the 1950s, a return to his traditional folk-blues roots made him one of the leading figures of the emerging American folk music revival and an international star. His long and varied career marks him as one of the key figures in the development of blues music in the 20th century.

[20] An American Folk musician, who was known for his energetic blues harmonica style, which frequently included vocal whoops and hollers and occasionally imitations of trains and fox hunts.

[21] An American Folk music singer and guitarist, best known for his collaboration with the harmonica player Sonny Terry.

²² Based on the true story of the 1827 Red Barn murder, a notorious 1827 murder committed in Suffolk. A young woman, Maria Marten, was shot dead by her lover William Corder. The two had arranged to meet at the Red Barn, a local landmark, before eloping to Ipswich. Marten was never seen alive again and Corder fled the scene. He sent letters to Marten's family claiming that she was in good health, but her body was later discovered buried in the barn after her stepmother spoke of having dreamed about the murder. Corder was tracked down in London, where he had married and started a new life. He was brought back to Suffolk and found guilty of murder in a well-publicised trial. In 1828, Corder was hanged at Bury St Edmunds in an execution witnessed by a huge crowd. The story provoked numerous newspaper articles, songs and plays. The village where the crime had taken place became a tourist attraction and the barn was stripped by souvenir hunters. The plays and ballads remained popular throughout the next century and continue to be performed today.

²³ The town itself now boasts seven pubs but has nine coffee shops.

²⁴ Built and named for the Empire Games (later, the Commonwealth Games) which were held in Cardiff in 1958. The City Council were initially reluctant to finance the new pool, but agreed to do so when confronted with the ultimatum of 'No Pool – No Games'.

²⁵ Now renamed the Bristol Beacon. The hall was formerly named after the slave trader, merchant and philanthropist Edward Colston, who founded Colston's School on the site in the early 18th century. It was renamed in 2020 after protests regarding Colston's ties to the Atlantic slave trade.

²⁶ The Wurzels are an English Scrumpy and Western band from Somerset, England, best known for their No 1 hit *The Combine Harvester* and the No 3 hit *I am a Cider Drinker* in 1976. They are known for using British West Country phrases such as 'ooh arr!' and calling young people 'young 'uns'. The name of the band was dreamt up by founder Adge Cutler. It is short for mangelwurzel, a crop grown to feed livestock, and wurzel is also sometimes used in the UK as a synonym for yokel.

Chapter 12 School

[1] This would have been a depot controlled by the Ministry of Agriculture which held supplies during WWII.

[2] A person born in Usk, or who has lived there for at least forty years, is known as an Usk Butterfly. The golden butterfly symbol was used by one branch of the Allgood family who, after a dispute, opened a separate branch of their Japanning company in Usk in 1763. The symbol distinguished their work, generally considered superior, from the Pontypool branch of the family. Japanning is a process which applies a brilliant hard lacquer to metal and the factory produced metal boxes, teapots, trays and other objects decorated with Japanese-style patterns on shiny black lacquer.

[3] School Attendance Officer

[4] Malted milk tablets are an old time retro candy favourite. These sweet treats are now called Malties. Horlicks tablets come in two flavours, natural or chocolate, both have a malted taste.

[5] Roger Edwards was a wealthy local merchant who lived at Allt-y-Bela, near Usk. Under his will of 1621, Edwards funded a free grammar school for Usk and almshouses. Teaching was originally carried on in Usk church but in 1836, the school was moved to Maryport Street and between 1843 and 1862 was enlarged and rebuilt, with the main body of the building on two storeys operating as the school and the smaller building to the north serving as a self-contained master's house. It is now a Grade 2 listed building. The school closed in 1956 and the building was then occupied by Monmouthshire County Council (MCC) as a community education centre. In 2010 the former Usk Grammar School Foundation, a charity administered by MCC, was returned to the control of local Trustees and renamed the Roger Edwards Educational Trust (REET).

Chapter 14 Neighbours

[1] Lionel Sweet was an internationally famous Usk fisherman. He was also a local councillor and a highly respected citizen of the town. Sweet won many fly casting competitions but the pride of place was in Scarborough 1953 when he became European Champion. He held the title for nearly 20 years.

The late Cyril Pearce, who was also a lifelong angler, said: 'As a kid I used to watch Lionel practise on the river Usk, where he would anchor saucer sized plastic plates 10 yards apart near the far bank and hit them with successive casts from the other side of the river. Such was his tremendous skill. Many showbiz stars of the day such as singer Frankie Vaughan came to Usk for his tuition, and stayed in the Three Salmons Hotel, much to the delight of the local ladies.'

When Usk's town clock was renovated, a timely secret was revealed during the process. Beneath the clock's dials, a plaque was found bearing the name *L. Sweet, 1932*. A further plaque printed in gold leaf read, *Repainted by L.T. Sweet, Usk - June 1964. Now 62 I don't suppose I shall do this next time, but I hope there are still salmon in the river.*

[2] Sweet's Fishing Tackle is one of the oldest retail establishments in Usk. The shop was opened in the 1930s by Harry Powell and then taken over by Lionel Sweet and his wife Molly. The late Cyril Pearce said, 'The shop run by Molly was a huge success, anglers came from far and wide to purchase Molly's hand-tied artificial flies.'

The shop was taken over by Lionel's assistant, Jean Williams and her husband in 1978, and is still going strong to this day. Past customers have included Sir Gareth Edwards, Billy Connolly, and Timothy Dalton.

Chapter 15 Folklore and Medicine

[1] This is used to treat a variety of skin disorders such as eczema, psoriasis, acne rosacea and acne.

[2] a small muslin-wrapped bag of synthetic ultramarine and sodium bicarbonate. Ultramarine is a very blue, blue and strangely enough (probably because it absorbs yellow light) clothes came out fantastically white. Its traditional use was also on bee stings, though folklore mentions its use for wasp stings too.

Chapter 16 Trostrey Characters and Eccentrics

[1] Bowyers was a greengrocers and fishmongers.

[2] The first line of the poem *Warning* by Jenny Joseph.

[3] Written by Herbert Rule and Harry Castling in 1924.

Chapter 17 Work

[1] Written by Paddy Ryan (Dr REW Fisher) written in 1938 when he was a medical student.

[2] An 'ancient' Irish ballad; it is complete with modal tune, simple story line, and inane refrain, but it differs from other ancient ballads in that it was written in 1950.

Printed in Great Britain
by Amazon